Other Books by Darwin Reid Payne

The Canterville Ghost
   (A Dramatization)
Design for the Stage: First Steps
Materials and Craft of the Scenic Model
A Christmas Carol
   (A Dramatization)
The Scenographic Imagination

Theory and Craft of the Scenographic Model
Revised Edition

Darwin Reid Payne

Southern Illinois University Press · *Carbondale and Edwardsville*

For Norman Young

Theory and Craft of the Scenographic Model is a revision of the text
originally entitled *Materials and Craft of the Scenic Model*, by Darwin
Reid Payne, copyright © 1976 by Southern Illinois University Press.

Revised edition copyright © 1985 by the Board of Trustees,
   Southern Illinois University
Printed in the United States of America
Edited by Teresa White
Designed by Gary Gore
Production supervised by Kathleen Giencke

91 90 89   4 3 2

Library of Congress Cataloging in Publication Data

Payne, Darwin Reid.
   Theory and craft of the scenographic model.

   Rev. ed. of Materials and craft of the scenic model. © 1976.
   Bibliography: p.
   Includes index.
   1. Theaters—Models. I. Payne, Darwin Reid.
Materials and craft of the scenic model. II. Title.
PN2091.M6P37 1985   792'.025'0228   84–5630
ISBN 0–8093–1193–3
ISBN 0–8093–1194–1 (pbk.)

Contents

vi Contents

Illustrations

Acknowledgments

Much of the material in this book deals with the visual and can be presented and understood only visually. I would like, therefore, to take this opportunity to express my gratitude to those photographers who have aided greatly in making that material comprehensible, especially to Elliott Mendelson, Myers Walker, and Bob Jones. A special debt is due to Elliott Mendelson for part 4 of this book in which he shares his thoughts on the problems of photographing scenographic models and outlines the skills needed when the photographer attempts to capture the three-dimensional spirit of the scenographic model in the two-dimensional image.

Introduction: Why the Scenographic Model?

This book is the second in a series of texts dealing with the art and craft of scenography. The earlier work, *Design for the Stage: First Steps*, and the subsequent revision of that text, *The Scenographic Imagination*, deal only with the conceptual basis of the scenographer's art; there the student is introduced to many of the principles and differing philosophies which underlie and inform the practice of scenography. The present work, while it cannot help but touch on theory and philosophy of scenic art, does not go deeply into esthetic matters. It is more concerned with the practicalities of scenic craftsmanship and in particular with the preparation of one of the scenographer's most helpful presentations, the scenographic model. But although this book is more or less limited to this one aspect of the scenographer's work, the tacit assumption will be that the principles of *The Scenographic Imagination* have been studied and absorbed and that the artistic directions suggested there will actively further all the techniques and skills the scenographer needs in the practice of his profession. Most importantly, he must constantly keep in mind that when art and craftsmanship are separated, not much remains of either one. And while other areas of scenic craftsmanship are barely touched on in this book, the need for their mastery by the student is patently assumed. It will not take long for the serious student to discover, however, that while texts are helpful in his education, they are only useful to the extent that they promote an active desire to experiment outside and beyond the guidelines set down here.

Modelmaking in general is an ancient and very human activity. It has been throughout the entire history of human endeavor central to the development of creative ideas. Horace Freeland Judson, in *The Search For Solutions*, correctly observes:

A model is a rehearsal for reality, a way of making a trial that minimizes the penalties for error. Playing with a model, a child can practice being in the world. Building a model, a scientist can reduce an object, a system, or a theory to a manageable form.

. . . modeling, however serious, enshrines an element of play. Watching a child, one turns that observation the other way around: for the child, absorbed in play, modeling has an essential aspect of seriousness—it's a way of grasping the way things are. For the scientist or engineer, conversely, the seriousness of modeling retains something of the youthful delight. Scientists are incessantly saying to each other "let's play around with that"—and modeling is the quintessential way of playing with the way things might work and might be. . . . Curiously, model-building can also be a way to create a theory. . . . *The performance of objects. The behavior of elaborate systems. A kind of theory-making. Modeling performs at these three levels.* (Italics mine)

The making of scale scenographic models is certainly not a new development in the theater. The scenographic model has been in existence as long as scenery itself; Leonardo da Vinci made scale working

1. *Seventeenth-century scenographic model from the court of Louis XIV*

adjunct to its theater practice. Some of the most elaborate models, such as the one shown in figure 1, created for the theatrical spectacles of Louis XIV's court, even went so far as to include carefully constructed proscenium arches. But even in the ordinary theaters of the time, models were prepared with great attention to precise detail, and a number of these models, the earliest dating from the middle of the seventeenth century, are preserved in many museums throughout the world. The Toneel Theater Museum in Amsterdam has an especially fine and in some ways unique collection of scenographic models from various ages of theater history (fig. 2).

While most scenographers continued to rely on graphic skills well into the nineteenth century—since design in the theater from 1660 on had been primarily a painter's art—models often accompanied the graphic sketch. The 1869 production for the Paris Opera's *Faust*, by Gounod, used both forms of communication (figs. 3, 4), but by the twentieth century, theatrical artists not only were using the scenographic model to facilitate production practice but also were employing these works as visual vanguards of revolutionary changes in theatrical theory. Both Gordon Craig's philosophy of a new more pure theater, and later Norman Bel Geddes's continuation of the Craig vision, were forcefully enshrined in scenographic model form (figs. 5, 6).

Nevertheless, notwithstanding this long history of scenographic model use, it has only been during the

models for the elaborate machines which figured importantly in the spectacles he was commissioned to design. In Shakespeare's time, the Revels Office provided paper models ("in the Italian style," reads a contemporary account) to the artisans who built and painted scenery for the elaborate court masques which also formed an important part of the Elizabethan theater. In fact, every period of theater history from the late Renaissance on has produced, with many examples still extant, scenographic models as a regular

2. Eighteenth-century scenographic model in the Toneel Theater Museum, Amsterdam

3. Scenographic sketch for Faust, 1869

past few decades that the making of the model has come into its own, has become central to the evolution of scenic exploration, and has all but superseded the making of scenic sketches. There are many reasons for this new emphasis, but perhaps the most important one is that the scenographers working in today's theater realize at last that the art they practice is not that of the painter but is an art of space, time,

and three-dimensional form. Very often the scenographer finds that the scenic sketch simply cannot show what is intended, that the scenographic model is the only real way to explore what will really happen in the theater. The whole trend of twentieth-century scenography has been, in fact, away from flats and painted drops and toward a stronger feeling for sculptural form. A host of new materials and construction techiques has made this trend both possible and economical; the old supremacy of illusory scene painting as the dominant feature of scenography has been successfully challenged. Add to this the ever-increasing use of kinetic scenery and the almost infinite possibilities which light and projection provide, and it is easy to understand why the single pictorial image has become less and less useful as a means of demonstrating what the scenographer can do on the stage. For these reasons, the scenographic model can often better show these newer trends and developments. There are, however, other very practical reasons why the student of scenography should master the skills needed to make these structures. Briefly, a few of these could be listed thus:

1. Scenographic modelmaking is a more comprehensible skill for the beginning student to develop than that of illusory painting. This is not to suggest that drawing and painting are not necessary skills for the scenographer; indeed, their mastery is absolutely essential to him. If, however, the student scenographer begins directly with those elements which more nearly touch the basic nature of his art—three-dimensional form, texture, space, and the effect of light on these elements—his progress is apt to be more rapid in other areas of visual art. Modelmaking can, in fact, serve as a focus for pursuing more graphic skills; drawing from the scenographic model, in fact, can greatly enhance the student's appreciation of the particular kind of space with which he must deal.

2. The scenographic model provides an image nearer to what can be realized on the actual stage than does the scenic sketch. Moreover, unlike a scenic sketch, models can be quickly viewed from more than one vantage point. Figure 7 shows a scenic drawing. It does have certain advantages; the nature of graphic materials allows the scenographer to make this work more atmospheric than most models can be. (Unless one is prepared to spend, as Norman Bel Geddes did for his *Divine Comedy* project [see fig. 6], much time, great sums of money, and is able to procure the ser-

6. *Scenographic model for* The Divine Comedy, *Norman Bel Geddes, 1921. Scene: Paradise, "O! Thou Sweet Light . . ." Norman Bel Geddes Collection, Theatre Arts Library, Harry Ransom Humanities Research Center, The University of Texas at Austin, by permission of Edith Lutyens Bel Geddes, executrix*

vices of a first-rate theatrical photographer like Bruguière.) A distinct advantage of a scenic drawing is that it can also indicate precise lighting effects; this aspect of a scenic drawing can be very helpful in either working out a desired lighting plot or indicating to a lighting designer (or to clarify for himself, if the scenographer is lighting his own production) a desired mood. And yet we are still limited to this one view; and that view is totally incapable of giving a true approximation of the three-dimensional space in which

7. *Scenographic sketch:* The Effect of Gamma Rays on Man-in-the-Moon Marigolds

the actual setting will exist. Figure 8 is a scenographic model of the same design. In some ways it it less "artful" than the sketch; the model is certainly less atmospheric. (It is perhaps worth noting that *no* scenic drawing ever makes it to the stage with all its painterly style and effect perfectly preserved; observe Eugene Berman's rendering of the act 2 setting for Verdi's *Rigoletto*, and then compare the actual setting of the stage, figs. 9, 10.) Nevertheless, the model does allow us to see what will really exist on the stage, what we can realistically expect to accomplish as a scenographer, and what we can lead others to expect from our work. In the long run, the scenographic model deludes us less about what is possible in the theater and sometimes leads us to solutions which we would not have encountered through the most extensive graphic experimentation. We can, in fact, view the model from any number of angles and discover possibilities not revealed from study of a flat single-perspective point of view (figs. 11, 12, 13). Scenographic models automatically force the scenographer to approach his design from the outset as a real structure which must be seen from virtually hundreds of vantage points, not as a picture viewed from one static point.

3. The scenographic model inherently provides more hard information for the various shops and technicians whose responsibility it is to build the actual setting. Not only does a model show how a com-

pleted setting will appear on the stage, it can also reveal that setting in its component units (see figs. 25, 26). Moreover, in the multiscene production it is of great necessity that the stage manager and technical director, in consultation with the scenographer, be able to plan and provide for the flow of traffic of the component parts of a setting, from scene change to scene change, in the most expeditious manner. The scenographic model reveals this information in a manner not possible to discover using graphic images alone. Further, models allow the scenographer to check more accurately the effect he intends against the limitations of the actual physical stage: sight lines, angles of viewing from audience positions, etc. Scenic sketches, with their easily achieved atmospheric effects and limitless possibility of form, tend to lull the scenographer into a false sense of what can be done in the real world of production. Of course, imagination should never be prematurely thwarted; but if the scenographer is not artistically equipped to deliver on the stage what he shows in his preliminary designs, he had best work in some other field of art. Besides, modelmaking is actually a stimulus to the imagination, not a limitation to it.

4. While precise lighting effects are difficult to obtain with a scenographic model, it does allow the scenographer (or independent lighting designer if the scenographer does not light the production himself) to better plan for the placement of lighting instru-

8. *Scenographic model:* The Effect of Gamma Rays on Man-in-the-Moon Marigolds

9. Scenographic sketch for Rigoletto, *by Eugene Berman*

10. Setting for Rigoletto, *by Eugene Berman*

ments in order to gain desired effects (fig. 14). The scenographer can, however, show the lighting designer precisely the areas and angles where light is necessary to best realize the visual effects originally intended. It is also possible, in making photographs of the scenographic model, not only to record a proposed design but also to show quite accurately how a design might be perceived in actual production (fig. 15) and to give a reasonably accurate impression of what will eventually be realized in performance.

5. A scenographic model invariably gives the director a much clearer view of how his own work will relate to the production as a whole. What most direc-

tors really want is not accomplished pictures of a static setting but indications as to how the space and forms the scenographer creates will further the production in performance. Peter Brook states the case succinctly: "a true theatre designer will think of his designs as being all the time in motion, in action, in relation to what the actor brings to a scene as it unfolds. *In other words, unlike the easel painter, in two dimensions, or the sculptor in three, the designer thinks in terms of the fourth dimension, the passage of time—not the stage picture, but the stage moving picture*" (italics mine). And the more we actually express our intentions in the third dimension, the easier it is to project those

intentions into that critical fourth which Brook thinks essential. This is, perhaps, the most important reason for making a model; to take that all-important step from the personal world of the imagination to show others that world in actual form, space, and material. Much misunderstanding can be prevented in the exploratory phase of production-planning by the use of carefully scaled models.

6. One last—but by no means least—advantage for making the scenographic model may, at first glance, seem a negative point: models often take more time to make than scenographic drawings. This longer period of time can be, however, a decided advantage to

the scenographer. And the reason for this is that quite often a scenographer's initial concept, expressed in quickly drawn sketches, is modified, deepened, and refined precisely because of the longer work period required in modelmaking. It is not uncommon, in fact, for the scenographer to change the whole form of a setting drastically (if not abandon entirely) without changing the basic ideas behind it, and in so doing improve his contributions to the final production when it appears in the theater. These changes are much better illustrated by the use of models than by scenographic sketches. In any case, they show the real changes in form, scale, and placement of critical act-ing areas more accurately than do drawings (figs. 16, 17). A beautiful drawing, it must be admitted, can be a powerful inducement for a director to accept a scenographer's early ideas; like the printed word, the well-defined artful image carries great authority. But it should also be kept in mind that getting one's way too soon is often more disastrous than not getting it at all.

These six reasons, then, should answer the question *"why the scenographic model."* Of course, different scenographers have differing views as to what the model should do and what techniques are most compatible with their mode of working. Most certainly, as the individual scenographer progresses in his career, the suggestions presented in the following pages will be modified, changed, and perhaps jettisoned altogether. That is only natural in the maturation of any artist. Nevertheless, it is hoped the information presented here will be of some primary value. If nothing else, it should provide those new to the craft and theory of scenographic modelmaking with a good point of departure; and beginnings are important in any field of endeavor. The most important point to remember about perfecting any craft, however, is that all the steps which go into it must be thoroughly understood conceptually as well as assimilated manually; skill is simply the hand doing what the mind tells it; accuracy, while it depends much upon practice, is also a state of mind. On the other hand, im-

13. Top view of model

portant as inspiration or a natural grasp of artistic problems is to the artist, he must also know how to build his product in much the same way as the cabinetmaker creates a piece of fine furniture or a baker makes a cake. Mastery of his craft cannot, unfortunately, assure the student a secure place in his profession; without it, however, he won't get many opportunities to acquire the recognition all artists desire.

Perhaps one last note of caution would not be out of place at this point. It touches on something which will always remain true for the scenographer using models in his work. Although not the only person to

14. *Scenographic model for* Incident at Vichy

15. *Production photograph of* Incident at Vichy

16. *Scenographic model:*
Suddenly Last Summer

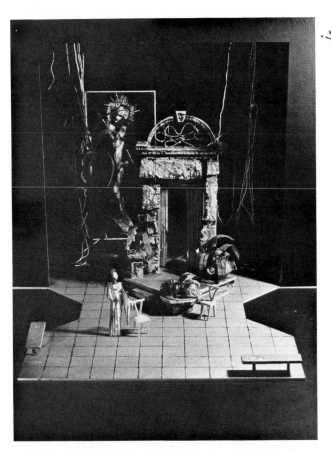

warn about the limitations of the scenographic model in the theater, Jean Cocteau has, perhaps, stated it more concisely than almost anyone else: "To reproduce a model too precisely on a stage is one of the greatest faults in theatrical craftsmanship." What he means, simply, is that it is a mistake not to recognize that relationships change—often drastically—as scales change, and that the scenographer must always keep his critical eye open to what those changes are and how they must be dealt with. He also meant that the model is only a step in the theatrical design process, not, as some scenic sketches do become, an artistic end in itself. As helpful as the model setting is—and it does have much to recommend it—it also has its own particular artistic dangers.

17. *Scenographic model:*
alternate variation of
Suddenly Last Summer

Part 1   *Basic Preparation*

1. Tools and Materials

Since we are most concerned in this book with demonstrating the mechanical skills and techniques the scenographer needs in modelmaking, it should be kept in mind that the mastery of these skills will always be greatly influenced by the tools and materials used. If they are inferior, outstanding results cannot be achieved; if they are well made and of quality, they will actively aid the scenographer in his development. Still, it is not necessarily true that the most expensive item is the best; nor is every tool available for modelmaking necessary. Few scenographers need all the tools listed in the various catalogues put out by manufacturers of drafting and modelmaking equipment. Those needed most are few and relatively inexpensive—especially if viewed as long-term investments. In fact, most of the scenographer's basic equipment will be serviceable for many years if given a modicum of care. But if he tries to "make do" with inferior tools and materials, such as the watercolor sets sold in the toy departments of inexpensive chain stores, or attempts to paint with a fifteen-cent brush on newsprint, he should not expect professional results from his efforts. For these reasons, recommendations as to specific types of tools and materials are suggested. Of course, it is to be expected that as each scenographer progresses in his career, he will develop affinities for certain kinds of tools and materials not included in the following pages. They may, in fact, totally contradict the recommendations made there. But the principle remains true for any item eventually replacing those suggested in this book: good tools conscientiously maintained and quality materials carefully selected can go far in helping the scenographer to use his time most effectively and insure for him the best possible transfer of his concepts into practical stage realities.

Basic Tools for Model Construction

Drawing Tools (Not Shown)

T square (at least 24 inches)
Triangles (30°–60° and 45°)
Architect scale (A flat scale with ¼ inch equals 1 foot and ½ inch equals 1 foot is a handier tool than the usual architect's scale.)
Mechanical pencil and sharpener
Compass (with an extension arm for making larger circles)
French curve or flexible curve maker

Model Construction Tools (Figure 18)

A. X-acto knife (slim barrel for No. 11 blade)
B. Razor saw (blades are interchangeable)
C. Steel edge (at least 18 inches) for guiding cutting edges

1

18. *Model construction tools*

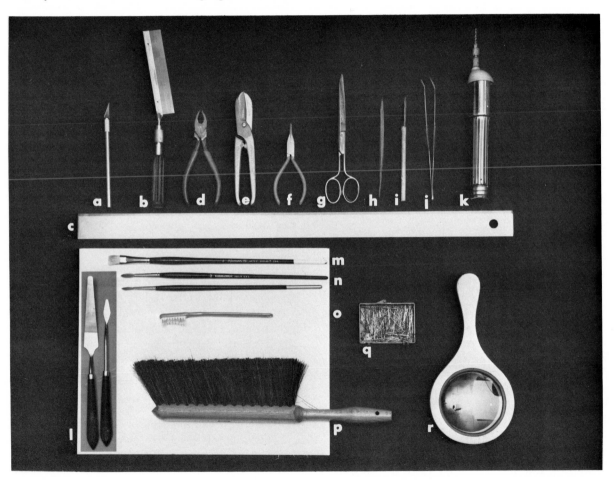

D. Small wire cutters
E. Small tin snips
F. Needle-nose pliers
G. Scissors
H. Small rat-tail file
I. Biology probe (for making small holes and holding pieces together while applying glue)
J. Biology tweezers (for handling small pieces)
K. Small battery-powered drill (with interchangeable bits)
L. Painting knives (for application and working of modeling paste)
M. Gesso brush (for application of gesso)
N. Sable watercolor brushes (for painting detail on exhibition models)
O. Toothbrush (for spattering paint effects on exhibition models)
P. Architect's cleaning brush (a necessity for keeping the modelmaking space clean of waste materials)
Q. Large dressmaker's pins (The larger the head, the easier the pin is to use and the easier on the fingertips. These pins do not bend as readily as lighter ones.)
R. Reducing glass (The opposite of a magnifying glass; it allows a work to be seen in a smaller dimension but with increased sharpness. Thus the larger outlines of the work are better revealed, while the details are reduced to a more subordinate proportion. This tool also aids the scenographer when making scenic sketches to get a fresh perspective on his work.)

NOTE: Throughout the text of this book a number of other tools and pieces of equipment will be introduced. Most of these should be considered as useful additions to the scenographer's basic tool kit. As the progress of the scenographer continues from student to professional practitioner, it should be expected that more sophisticated tools will become necessary; these will be introduced at appropriate points in the text when questions of professional practice arise. Many of these, it should also be expected, will be beyond the financial capability—or real need—of the student during the basic training period, which is the primary focus of this book.

Materials for Model Construction (Figure 19)

A. Various paper boards, thinner papers, foils, and textiles
B. Balsa woods of various sizes
C. Styrofoam pieces
D. Wire screening and meshes of various weaves
E. Wire, metal pieces, and plates
F. Found objects (twigs, chain, rusted metal pieces, prefabricated forms, etc.)
G. Found images

NOTE: Hobby and art supply stores carry balsa

19. *Materials for model construction*

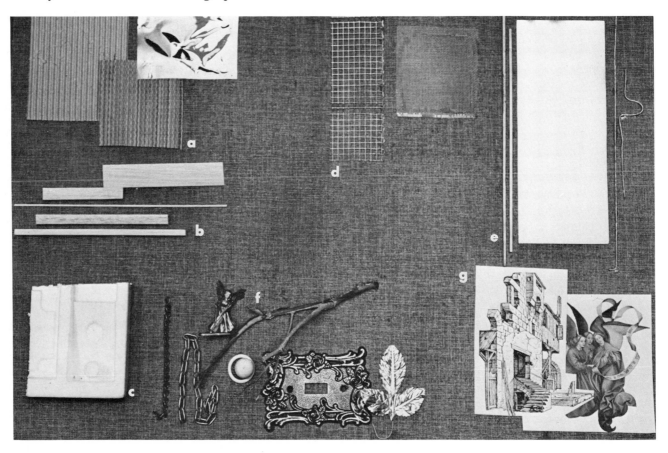

woods and traditional modelmaking supplies. Recently they have also begun to stock small metal rods and pipes of various dimensions as well as metal plates; these can be obtained in several types of metal: brass, aluminum, chrome plate, etc. Wire screening and meshes are obtainable at building supply or hardware stores.

Materials for Assembly and Finishing Models (Not Shown)

Gesso
Modeling paste
Plastic sand (available from paint supply stores)
Masking tape
Duco cement (recommended above all others)
Rubber cement
Elmer's glue (the best of the white glues)
Inks (sepia and black)
Tempera paints (all basic colors)
Water-soluble metallic colors (This is a relatively new product and comes in a variety of finishes: gold, silver, copper, brass, etc. Regular metallic paints are not recommended for use on exhibition models except, in some instances, metallic sprays.)
Tube watercolors (for more transparent painted effects on exhibition models)
Metallic paste (This is a product that is not water-soluble. These finishes—gold, silver, copper, brass—can be used to enrich and add highlights to the textured surfaces of an exhibition model. See part 2, section 7, under "Finishing the Exhibition Model.")
Various aerosol spray paints, stains, and sealers
NOTE: An airbrush is a helpful, although rather expensive, tool. It allows the scenographer to substitute water-soluble paints for painting basic coats on the model. It is also a more refined method of obtaining shaded effects than possible with aerosol spray products.

2. The Scenographer's Work Space

Doubtless no two artists could be expected to have identical work patterns; the individual manner in which each works, therefore, probably accounts more for the great variation one encounters from studio to studio than for architectural differences. Nevertheless most studios could be expected to have certain features in common.

Practically all artists find that the place they work has a definite effect on the kind of work they do; partly in the amount they are able to produce and also in the quality of that work. And the deeper they become involved in their profession, the more particular they are about not only the tools and materials of their craft but also where these are employed. To the working scenographer, organization of his work area is not a restrictive activity; it is one that allows him to advance most freely. But what are some of those work needs? How are they expressed in work areas? Some of these needs one would almost certainly encounter in most studios would be:

1. A place to think, make rough sketches, confer with others concerned with the production.

2. A place to make finished sketches: watercolor, pastel, pen and ink, etc. (with a water supply near this area if possible).

3. A place to create and experiment with models and to be able to work with three-dimensional materials.

4. A place to make large-sheet working drawings (a drafting table).

5. Storage areas for reference books (shelving); file clippings, catalogues, etc. (file cabinets); working drawings (flat files); sketches and set drawings (flat files or racks); drawing materials, drafting supplies, model materials (shelving, chests); finished models (shelving); slides and projections (slide files).

6. Display areas for current ideas, notes, schedules, etc., near working areas (bulletin boards).

7. A projection screen on which to show slides and a permanent setup for projector.

8. An all-purpose worktable on which to lay out work in progress, draw up full-scale details, etc.

(All these areas should have general lighting from the studio's overall illumination, but should also have specifically directed light sources in each individual area.)

9. And, although not an absolute necessity, provision for refreshment—an area for coffee-making, etc.—and marginal entertainment—phonograph, radio. A scenographer spends a great deal of time in his studio; although it is a working place, it should be as comfortable as he can make it.

After only a few years, most scenographers find they need additional storage space for past projects (or for materials they might not need to use very often). The working scenographer, therefore, should examine his studio from time to time and store in some other place all the things he does not absolutely need. Nothing is quite as exasperating as trying to put together a complicated production and having its component parts constantly being lost in a welter of past projects or unimportant materials. Few professional designers can afford the luxury of being unorganized. Figure 20 is a drawing that incorporates these work necessities into a workable studio layout:

A. Study and conference area
B. Storage for drafting materials and art supplies
C. Drafting table—immediate reference materials and supplies kept in shelving above
D. Bulletin board

E. Sketching and model building area
F. Storage shelving for models
G. File cabinets
H. Flat file cabinets
I. Projection screen (pulls down when used)
J. Book shelving
K. All-purpose worktable
L. Slide storage
M. Slide projector

NOTE: Two useful pieces of equipment (fig. 21), although relatively expensive, are a tabletop slide viewer (A) that allows perusal of a series of slides—up to forty at a time—in ordinary light and an opaque projector such as the one shown (B). An opaque projector is useful in converting small images into larger ones which can then be traced for full-scale use in the scenic shop. The duplication of both line drawings or fully painted images without preliminary drawing by the scenographer makes this piece of equipment very useful in the studio. (35-mm slides can also be used for duplicating small images which have been photographed; see part 3, section 12 for further discussion of this practice.)

Modelmaking almost invariably requires more work space than that for rendering scenic sketches or making working drawings. Also, the number of materials and tools is greater and requires more ample storage space. While a single working area can be used for almost all the projects a scenographer needs to make,

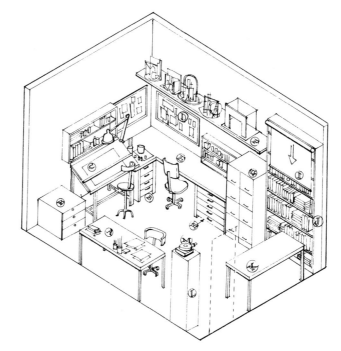

20. *The scenographer's work space*

if at all possible, *keep areas which have different working requirements separate.* For instance, the drafting area should never be used for any great amount of cutting or painting: the surface of the table needed for making accurate working drawings will become permanently damaged very quickly if used in such a way. In fact, the work area for modelmaking takes a great

21. A, *35-mm slide viewer;* B, *opaque projector*

deal of punishment and should have a surface impervious to the materials and tools which could render a drafting table unusable. Figure 22 shows the specific area a modelmaker might arrange in the studio for an efficient work pattern. As with other parts of the studio, lighting is extremely important; more than one source is required with the brightest amount of light coming from in front of the area where detailed work is to be done. The shadowless light of fluorescent fixtures is especially helpful in modelmaking; making accurate cuts in materials such as illustration board is difficult if hard shadows are cast by the cutting guide.

A. Basic work area. This surface should be covered with a strong material such as formica which resists scarring and can be easily cleaned or materials accidentally spilled on it.

B. Removable working board. Even though the general worktable is constructed to withstand hard usage, an expendable material should be used for cutting, gluing, and texturing model parts. One-half-inch plywood, untempered masonite, or heavy illustration board is suitable and makes it economically feasible to change this surface at regular intervals.

C. Vertical storage of flat materials. These would include illustration board, bristol board, acetate, etc.

D. Storage for basic supplies of materials not needed for immediate use.

E. The model stage (see part 2, section 5, for details of construction). This unit should be kept in close proximity to the working area so that model pieces can be quickly tested for size, scale, and placement.

F. Shelf storage for materials constantly in use. These would include gesso, modeling paste, paint, pins, adhesives, etc.

G. Racks for balsa materials. Display of these materials not only keeps them unbroken and available, it also keeps the scenographer aware of what is in short supply.

H. Pegboard for tools constantly in use. Nothing is as exasperating as looking for a specific tool and not being able to locate it. This type of display unit makes it easy to find a tool and then gives a place to return it when no longer needed.

I. Bulletin board. A scenographer simply cannot

22. *Scenographic model
building area*

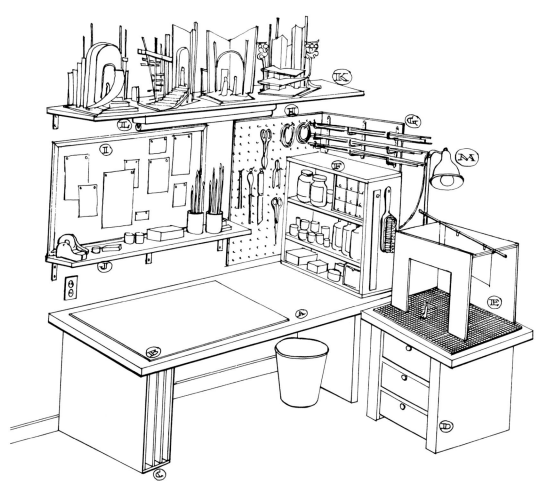

23. *Suggested graphics work area*

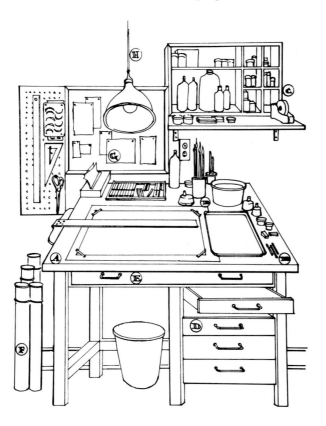

function properly without an ample area on which to display all the notes and images that remind him of the various facets of the projects being worked on.

J. A shelf immediately above the working area helps keep small items and materials out of the way or from being misplaced. Modelmaking often requires a number of processes being worked on at the same time, usually involving a large number of materials and tools. Great frustration can be avoided by keeping the immediate working area orderly.

K. The best place to keep completed models is on shelving up and out of the immediate work area of the studio. It does help to have them, however, within close range for reference.

L. General lighting fixture above and in front of the work area. Warm-toned fluorescent light is probably best for this purpose because it is virtually shadowless and does not glare.

M. A small incandescent lamp above the model stage unit is useful not only because it illuminates but also because it makes possible the viewing of the model under the effect of directed light. Although, at best, this use of light can give only crude approximations, the information it imparts can be helpful.

Suggested Graphics Work Area (Figure 23)

A. Overall work surface. This surface should be covered with replaceable drafting-table material. (This material is usually light green with white backing and has a relatively soft front surface). A good drafting-table surface can be quickly and permanently ruined if left uncovered. The nature of the covering material, moveover, is such that any drafting done on it is improved in line quality. It is also advisable to keep a large roll of brown paper to be used over this covering when painting scenic sketches, paint schedules, etc. Covering the entire working surface with this paper is particularly necessary when using good pastels; the dust from these soft materials tends to spread over anything not covered.

B. Immediate materials and tools area. Keeping equipment in easy reach in some known order is such an obvious recommendation that few instructors make it. Nevertheless, it is important that such a recommendation be made; instrument and materials layout is a carefully planned procedure in a hospital operating room and is taught in medical schools. While the consequences of sloppy procedure in a scenographer's studio are certainly not as devastating as they would be in an operating room, a haphazard approach to a project can have a definite effect on the quality of the work being done.

C. Storage of expendable materials. These materials should be kept in immediate proximity to the working area but not in it. Open shelving is the most effective way in which to see what you have and what you need. Nothing is more exasperating than running out of material with only one drawing to make or one sketch to finish.

D. Storage for permanent tools. A scenographer's tools and instruments do much of the work for him. They should be of good quality and carefully maintained. Part of that maintenance is providing proper storage, which is easily obtainable from a myriad of units individually designed for practically every kind of tool or need. Investment in these storage units is sound inasmuch as it extends the life of tools and prevents their loss.

E. Storage for flat materials and finished flat work. Flat storage is essential to the professional scenographer. Most drafting tables have immediate storage for drafting paper in the table itself. It is also possible to obtain (although usually quite expensive) individual drawers which stack as new flat storage is acquired.

F. Mailing tubes for past production working drawings. The most effective means of storing working drawings for past productions is in mailing tubes. (These come in various lengths and diameters. Drafting supply houses also stock architectural drawing storage tubes.)

G. Bulletin board over working area. In most working scenographer's studios an important feature is a place to put up images, materials, notes, schedules, etc., directly in view. At times the materials put there are necessary to the immediate problems of a project; at other times these materials simply act as inspirational nonspecific reminders. In any case, this everchanging display area is an important part of the graphics working space.

H. Lighting of the work area. This is a most important consideration in the planning of a studio. General light should be provided throughout the entire area, and specific light should be carefully placed so that one does not work in shadow. The quality of light is a question of individual taste; incandescent bulbs give a warmer light but also cast relatively hard shadows; fluorescent light gives fewer shadows but distorts color. Manufacturers of fluorescent lighting, however, do provide means for changing the color quality of the natural light from such sources. Recent studies have shown that there is a direct correlation between hyperactivity and fluorescent light; many of those who work in this kind of light tend to show higher levels and tendencies to experience quicker fatique. The lighting of a studio is of prime importance to the work done in it; great care should be given to just what is the best for the individual using such an area.

Basic Tools and Materials for Graphic Work (Not Shown)

1. Permanent drafting equipment: T square; triangles; architectural scales (flat scales, while having few scales, are preferable to triangular scales, but harder to find); straight edges; templates and curves; flexible curves; mechanical pencils; mechanical pencil sharpeners; mechanical drawing tools (compass, inkers); rapidograph pens; drafting brush.

2. Expendable drafting materials: tracing papers; erasers; drafting tapes; leads.

3. Permanent tools for scenic sketches: brushes; watercolor pallettes; porcelain tray (preferable to plastic mixing trays); water container.

4. Expendable materials for scenic sketches: illustration boards; drawing pads; inexpensive paper; tube watercolors; tempera; metallic colors; inks; pastels; Conte crayons; drawing pencils; fixative; tissue.

5. Collage and assemblages: found images; found flat materials which could include metal foils, flat-textured materials (cloth, plastic, etc.), string; glues-binders (white glue, cement, gesso, modeling paste).

3. Types of Scenographic Models

The Experimental Model

The experimental model is not so much a type of model as it is an activity (fig. 24). Often the scenographer will begin to search for a design concept with three-dimensional forms and materials directly on a scaled model stage. He does not, when working in this manner, first draw out a predetermined design and then build a scale replica of it. Rather, he usually cuts out and assembles materials and objects with

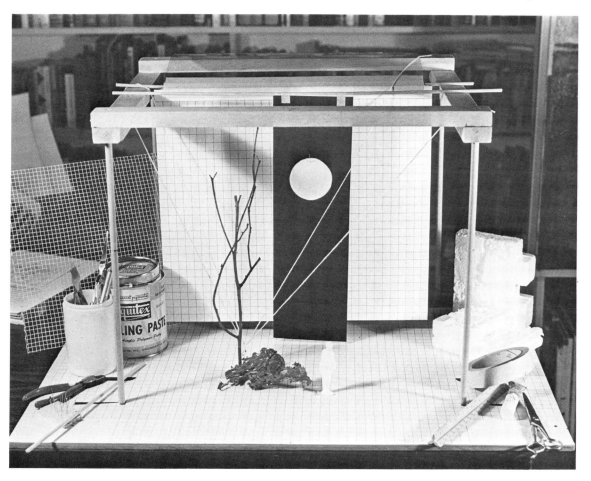

24. *The experimental model*

little regard as to measurement or scale. The object of this activity is, as its name implies, to determine scenic ideas in an experimental way rather than to think them out beforehand conceptually or on paper. This activity is meant to begin the creative process in a more direct manner than sketching would allow; it also relies heavily on the scenographer's intuitive ability to see possibilities in accidental results. It is, in fact, nothing much more than creative play—but with an eventual purpose. It is possible for the scenographer to create accidental and random arrangements which could lead to a solution when, in the formative stages of a design concept, he finds himself at an impasse. A variety of materials can be used in this experimental model—wire mesh and screening, metal foils, plastics, modeling clay, photographic images, fabrics, string, styrofoam, etc.—as well as the traditional illustration board, heavy paper, and balsa wood. The scenographer should also keep in mind that in the present-day theater practically any form or texture used in these models can be duplicated in full scale on the stage in any number of lightweight materials and so he should not be afraid of being "impractical" in his choice of exotic forms or materials. It is advisable, however, that the human scale always be present in these models (as, indeed, with all scenic models); this is easily remembered if a scale figure is constantly kept on the model stage.

The Working Model

The working model's primary function is to show how the exact form of the setting will appear onstage. It is usually evolved from experimental model possibilities. The working model, however, must be as accurate in working detail as possible. This model is almost always finished with a coat of gesso so that the various materials used—balsa, illustration board, wire, etc.—will have a common surface finish and tonality; this makes it easier to see the total form of the setting without the distraction of differing materials (fig. 25).

Occasionally, scenographers may draft onto the working model architectural details in pencil, although this is a more common practice when making the lightweight bristol board model. It is also a common practice to construct the working model in the actual units which will be used in the full-scale setting (fig. 26).

This approach helps the shops not only to study the construction requirements of the individual units but also to understand how they will be assembled, separated, and stored when the setting is actually in the theater during a performance.

Working models also often help to solve problems which cannot be understood or fully tested by graphic means or mathematical calculation alone. The empir-

25. *A working model:*
Arsenic and Old Lace

26. *A working model (in
component parts)*

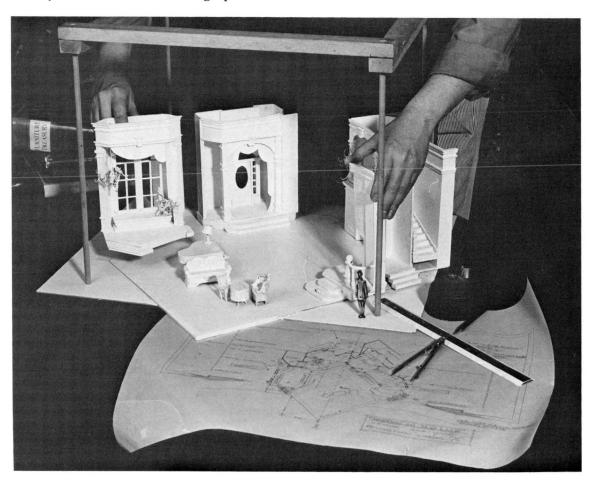

ical approach—a "rehearsal for reality," as Horace Freeland Judson has called it—has become widespread in all fields of experimentation; from genetic engineering to economic three-dimensional forecasts; from attempting to understand molecular structure to determining flow patterns in waterways. Extensive use of models to obtain technical information serves identical purposes in the theater; to discover the ways structures behave in motion, to seek out stress points or possibly dangerous situations, as well as to better determine how complex systems work, all of these can be predicted by working models.

In 1981, the San Francisco Opera decided to produce Jean-Pierre Ponnelle's staging of Aribert Reiman's *Lear*. Immediately great technical problems arose. The production was first performed in the relatively modern highly mechanized National Theater in Munich, West Germany, a theater with an extensive built-in hydraulic system, a system on which Ponnelle's design was based. The problems presented by reproducing the original design in the older, less well equipped San Francisco house were such that they would only be explored and solved by experimentation with an accurate working model of the mechanisms necessary to make the design work in this different theater. John Priest, the resident technical director of the San Francisco Opera, along with Larry Klein and Noel Uzemack, constructed a large working model to test the viability of the lifts needed to raise the various sections of the setting. The model shown in figure 27 was greatly responsible for the successful resolution to the problems that transference of Ponnelle's design from one theater to another created.

The working model, therefore, is more a means to an end than something to be shown as a work of art; often these constructions do not survive their usefulness in the scenic shop (where they are often made by the technical staff, not the scenographer himself) and are rarely kept by the scenographer as he might those works which comprise our next category of scenographic model: the exhibition model.

The Exhibition Model

The exhibition model (fig. 28), unlike the working model, is completely finished; that is, it is painted as nearly as possible to show the color and treatment of the scenic units as they are to appear on the stage. As its name suggests, it is purposefully made to be shown and, like scenic sketches, often assumes an artistic value beyond its usefulness as working information for scenic technicians. While the working model is usually made to come apart so that the shifting routine of the actual setting can be studied, the exhibition model is often (but not always) built as a solid unit. Often a scenographer will not take the time to complete a model such as this; it does require consid-

27. *A working model for*
Lear

erably more time while adding little more information than that given by the working model. Nevertheless, if the scenographer is interested in "selling" a particular idea or wants to make quite sure those working on the actual setting understand just how he wants the final product to appear, nothing is quite as persuasive as this type of model.

NOTE: Part 2, section 7 (see "Finishing the Exhibition Model"), discusses additional techniques and materials necessary for this type of model.

28. *An exhibition model:* La
Bohème

Part 2 *The Craft of Scenographic Modelmaking*

4. The Basic Phases

While it is not probable that all scenographers will follow exactly the same steps in planning a production, the process of making the scenographic model does by necessity have certain fundamental lines of development. The two most basic phases of this process are as follows:

The Conceptual Stage: Ideas

All work in the theater starts as an idea, a concept without physical form. The scenographic model is no exception. However, it would be a mistake to believe that the transition from an idea or a feeling to a finished design is a single step; many steps, in fact, intervene and the process is, if anything, complex and multifaceted.

Probably the most often asked question of any scenographer is, "Where do your ideas come?" The real answer is quite simple: everywhere. But explaining the answer is somewhat more difficult, and the entire process can never be fully revealed (and some aspects of the answer remain shadowy even to the scenographer himself). Nevertheless, while it is an actual truth that the scenographer does obtain what he needs in his work from literally everywhere, it is difficult to dispell the myth that the artist relies pri-

marily on that intangible property of the mind we designate as *imagination*. What is difficult to explain to anyone is that while imagination is required in the practice of any art, its real role in the creative process is to select, judge, reject, and synthesize the materials found in the research of external facts and images. As the eighteenth-century painter, Sir Joshua Reynolds, forcefully reminds us: "The greatest natural genius cannot subsist on its own stock; he who resolves never to ransack any mind but his own will soon be reduced from mere barrenness to the poorest of all imitations. It is vain to invent without materials on which the mind may work and from which invention must originate. Nothing can come of nothing."

All artists, and not least the scenographer, are included in this important dictum. *Even the greatest minds*, is no idle phrase; for some our own century's most important theater figures have relied heavily on the work of not only those who lived in the past but their contemporaries as well. Bertolt Brecht, certainly one of the greatest innovators of the twentieth century, often used the work of others in ways which might surprise those who believed that his plays sprang full-blown from the esoteric levels of his own individual imagination. One example—although not unique in the career of Brecht—should reveal the somewhat blatantly direct manner in which the creative mind works:

In his part-folk, part-modern parable play, *The Cau-*

casian Chalk Circle, Brecht required that the setting for the wedding scene in part 3 should include a small enclosure that, during the playing of the scene, would gradually fill up with festive guests. In figure 29 we see the setting designed by Karl von Appen for the original Berliner Ensemble production. As a production photograph of this scene shows, the characters literally fill this structure from wall to wall (fig. 30). Brecht meant the scene to be a comic one and instructed his scenographer accordingly. But what very few in the audience watching the play knew was that the visual source for this scene was a sequence in the 1935 Marx Brothers motion picture, *A Night at the Opera* (fig. 31). This is where Brecht got the inspiration which was crucial to the designing of the setting for the scene. Doubtlessly von Appen also found it necessary to do other research; research that provided him images such as the one shown in figure 32, a painting by the early fifteenth-century Flemish Limbourg brothers for a book of hours (a private prayer book of the period). This kind of historical research was also necessary to support the time period during which Brecht set his play. But the fact remains that the real impetus for the scenographer's design came from a 1930s' Hollywood farce. Brecht was one of the first in the modern theater to demonstrate to us that ideas may come from *any* period and from *any* source as long as they are used to support the playwright's dramatic concepts and that historical accuracy is

sometimes counterproductive to the staging of plays set in other times. Since Brecht and his scenographers first formulated the theatrical philosophy of *conscious anachronism*, this mode of thought has become one of the most widespread practices in the production of plays and the design of scenery and costume.

It is also interesting to observe in figure 30 how closely Brecht, in his actual staging of the wedding scene in *The Caucasian Chalk Circle*, took the positioning and grouping of the performers suggested by the scenographer in his scenic sketch. This does indicate that while the initial idea of the scene was Brecht's, he allowed others to aid in the development of that basic idea in production; in fact, Brecht himself often wrote that he counted heavily on his scenographers to flesh out his sometimes sketchy suggestions.

Let us examine another external source which was in great part responsible for a design on the stage. Figure 33 shows a setting for David Storey's play, *Home*. Here we see a frankly theatrical, almost abstract stage arrangement; but this design is, in point of fact, an almost direct copy of an image found outside the theater in the actual world (fig. 34). And this is the very photograph the scenographer used in his research for the play: a long narrow path in an English park with its final destination lost in the distant winter fog. But, in actuality, this image was not decided upon immediately but only *after* the scenographer began a search

29. *Scenographic sketch for* The Caucasian Chalk Circle

for such an image that was first suggested by a work that seemed to graphically sum up all the thoughts and feelings Storey wrote into his play: a sonnet by Shakespeare:

That time of year thou mayst in me behold
When yellow leaves, or none, or few, do hang
Upon those boughs which shake against the cold,
Bare [ruin'd] choirs where late the sweet birds sang.
In me thou seest the twilight of such day
As after sunset fadeth in the west,
Which by and by black night doth take away,
Death's second self that seals up all in rest.
In me thou seest the glowing of such fire
That on the ashes of his youth doth lie,
As the death-bed whereon it must expire,

Consum'd with that which it was nourish'd by.
    This thou perceiv'st, which makes thy love more strong,
    To love that well which thou must leave ere long.

There are literally no limits to the ways a scenographer can use his findings, as the setting shown in figure 35—a French production for the play *Rabelais*—demonstrates. Here the scenographer took his entire inspiration from a single image in a medical textbook printed during the period that Rabelais actually lived (fig. 36). This image was then reproduced on the stage as a grossly enlarged structure that was variously used as a banquet table, a platform, and for numerous other purposes as the play progressed.

Rarely, however, does the scenographer literally reproduce any image in its entirety on the stage. More likely, elements of the original source will be used selectively. While the model for *Cat on a Hot Tin Roof* (fig. 37), owes its inspiration to the image shown in figure 38, the source was used primarily as a suggestive catalyst to the imagination, not as a literal guide for naturalistic reproduction.

It is easy to see, therefore, that a scenographic idea often has strange history and that an idea or an image for a scenographic design rarely comes from one source alone or from one branch of arts exclusively. It would be more accurate to say that what finally appears in the theater is an amalgam of *all* human activities, all arts and crafts, and is gleaned from all possible research sources. But the main point to be observed here—and we will, in later sections of this book, explore more deeply this question of the sources of imagination—is that in the initial stages of seeking out a beginning point for the creation of a scenographic design, there is really no limit to the images or ideas available to the scenographer for his use; nor should the scenographer ever arbitrarily restrict his search to those from his own mind or to those of the playwright. It must also be remembered that it is the

32. Fifteenth-century Flemish painting

imagination's chief function to synthesize images from the outside world into physical realities on the stage that best serve the total production, not to demonstrate the scenographer's artistic prowess.

When, after some image is found or a visual idea occurs to the scenographer, a number of options lie open to him as he begins to put these ideas into phys-

33. *Scenographic sketch for*
Home

34. *Initial image for design
of* Home

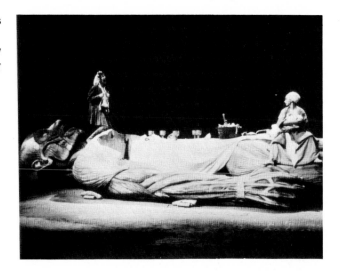

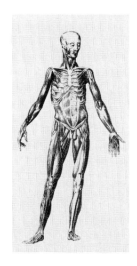

ical form. Many scenographers assemble sketches and images onto collagelike boards before proceeding with actual three-dimensional experimentation. (Later we will see one example where the design was entirely derived from the assembly of Xerox images into a flat collage design which was then translated into a three-dimensional structure with very little change: part 3, section 10). On the other hand, the scenographer may begin his work directly with actual three-dimensional materials—found objects, boards and papers, wire

screening and meshes, cord, etc.—without any prior graphic work. (In part 3 we will examine in greater detail the wide latitude this form of working affords.) But, as the student scenographer will probably discover very early in his study, the development of most ideas into scenographic form means that a great deal of both kinds of work—graphic and three-dimensional—must take place; that rarely does one kind of work ever take entire precedence over the other, and that often the one kind of work invariably leads to the other and then back again much in the way one

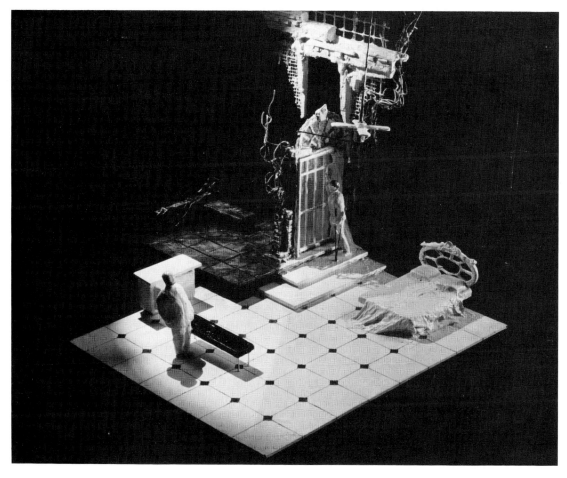

38. *Ruined plantation house*

plays leapfrog. By that I mean that rarely is any art-work a straight-line activity with clearly defined steps, one following the other in a strict order of cause and effect. Modelmaking, like all other art-work, tends to proceed in stages each made up of differing (not always predictable) forms of experimentation. A sketch might precede an experiment on the model stage or it might just be a graphic record of what is assembled there. But it is also possible that that sketch might, in turn, cause the scenographer to alter on the model something suggested by the sketch. And this process may take place dozens of times before a viable solution to a design problem for a particular scene finally occurs. The scenographer will doubtlessly find that as he works on project after project it becomes increasingly difficult to seprate his work into neat self-contained steps. The professional scenographer must be expert in all forms of artwork and must continually develop that outer eye which can capitalize on the rich visual world which surrounds us all.

I would not like to leave the impression that all scenographic design is simply a matter of finding a striking image to copy or the cannibalization of the creative work of others; obviously that is not so. The imagination is also capable of visualizing original concepts—although almost always based on some aspects of the objective world—from which a design will develop. Before the actual work on a production begins, before the scenographer starts his own experimentation or the director begins to rehearse his performers, most productions are thoroughly discussed so that certain agreed-upon intellectual and visual directions will be correctly charted. Often the scenographer and the director working together—using the written images of the playwright or the librettist—will create their own imagery; imagery they believe will best serve that of the text or libretto. Read, for instance, these words of the noted British scenographer John Bury concerning the Royal Shakespeare Company's *The Wars of the Roses*, a group of Shakespeare's related historical plays that were performed as a unit:

The Wars of the Roses was designed in steel—the steel of the plate armour—the steel of the shield and the steel of the broadsword.

In this hard and dangerous world of our production, the central image—the steel of war—has spread and forged anew the whole of our medieval landscape. On the flagged floors of sheet steel tables are daggers, staircases are axe-heads, and doors the traps on scaffolds. Nothing yields: stone walls have lost their seduction and now loom dangerously—steel-clad—to enclose and to imprison. The countryside offers no escape—the danger is still there in the iron foliage of the cruel trees and, surrounding all, the great steel cage of war.

The costumes corrode with the years. The once-proud red rose of Lancaster becomes as a rusty scale on the soldiers' coats; the milk-white rose of York is no more than a pale blush on the tarnished steel of the Yorkist insurrection. Colour drains and drains from the stage until, among the drying patches of scarlet blood, the black night of England settles on the leather costumes of Richard's thugs.

Certainly, the mature scenographic imagination is at work here even though what is discussed is nothing more than a list of materials, objects, and literal descriptions of the effects of war and the passage of time.

The Construction of the Final Model

Once definite ideas are formulated, a number of operations must be performed:

1. Drafting of the floor plan onto a base plane. Usually this base is the heaviest material—or as heavy as any material—in the model. One-hundred-weight cold press illustration board is probably the best material for this base regardless of the type of model being made. Anything of less substance will usually warp; if this happens, nothing placed on it will stand straight. Heavier materials, such as plywood or masonite, are overkill; also their surfaces do not respond to art materials such as watercolor, tempera, or inks as well as illustration board does.

2. Drafting the component parts of the model. This

is done by the same techniques and procedures employed in making regular front elevations for working drawings. The only difference is that the drafting is done on whatever material will be used in the model; the weight in large part determines the type of model being made.

3. Cutting and assembly of the parts into scenic units. For working models, these units will correspond directly to the units made in the scenic shop.

4. Application of textures and three-dimensional detail to the basic units. Paper models will have this detail indicated by graphic means; more finished models and exhibition models will require other materials for their completion: gesso, modeling paste, glued-on textures, etc.

5. Final finish of the model. For the paper model, graphic work completes it; for the working model, the gesso coat is the last step; for the exhibition model, a number of steps follow the gesso coating—painting, shading, highlighting, are all necessary for this model, as well as are detailed set dressing and scale representations of the performers.

(Below, we will be examining in greater detail all the steps encompassed in these two phases of model-making. But, before proceeding directly to the specific techniques of model building, let us examine a very important piece of equipment necessary to the whole craft of scenic models: the model stage unit.)

5. The Model Stage Unit: Its Construction and Use

It is taken for granted that all designers need an ability to sketch an idea on paper quickly. These drawings, often crude and sketchy, are usually diagrammatic and reveal only the most basic form of the intended design. Many professional scenographers will even admit that they make their exhibition drawings after the actual design has been realized on the stage. These scenographers frankly state they do not have time to make detailed set drawings before that time. What then does take precedent over elaborate renderings? In many instances experimentation on the model stage is the answer. In fact, it is not uncommon for the scenographer to begin almost directly with three-dimensional work although, as we have said, almost all do commit their very first thoughts to paper in small, quickly drawn diagrams. Figure 39 shows such a unit with a model being constructed within its boundaries.

For many scenographers this approach is more productive than a strictly pictorial one. And while it might be thought that the model is a product which has been completely worked out on paper before its construction, such is rarely the case. The real value of the model stage unit lies in the opportunities it affords the scenographer to test ideas before giving

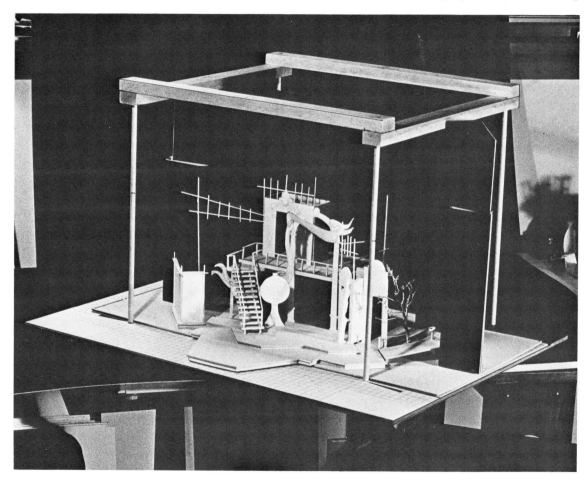

the scenic model its final form. In fact, the scenographer who uses the model stage often does not begin making working drawings for final scenic sketches until after he has satisfied himself with the shape and form of the set he has worked out experimentally on this stage.

This unit, therefore, to be of any real value, must be constructed as a type of instrument which can immediately reveal the placement of objects and structural units quickly and accurately in known scale. The floor of such a unit should be a grid system which allows for an immediate reading of anything placed on it. Figure 40 is a diagram of a model stage unit in its simplest form.

It is not difficult or expensive to build a unit similar to the one shown; even with hand tools, it can be constructed fairly quickly using the diagram given here as a guideline. While basically a simple structure, other features found on the actual full-scale stage can be included: line-sets noted both on the floor and on the top sidebars, removable traps, masking, etc. Most professional scenographers have a unit similar to this (some more complicated than others) in their studios and make constant use of it in their work. In Richard Pilbrow's book, *Stage Lighting*, page 49 contains a model stage unit complete with fly loft and counterweights as well as a working electrical system (fig. 41). Few scenographers need (or could afford) such a setup. In fact, Jo Mielziner, who had just such a model stage in the 1930s, candidly admitted sometime later that precise lighting problems simply could not be worked out on this type of unit with any degree of accuracy, that his own stage was not much more than a rather elaborate toy which, although a great deal of fun, produced definitely limited results. While the unit recommended here is elemental, it will provide the scenographer with good workable information, actively suggesting configurations and alternatives he would never discover with only pen or pencil.

While objects placed on the floor grid can be immediately read in terms of size and placement at ground level, those images or objects which exist above the floor level are not as easily put into an accurate context. There is a device, however, which will allow the scenographer to place a number of images into various relationships—both to the model stage structure as well as to each other—which can be accurately measured. The device is simple and consists of two basic parts. One part consists of a number of clear acetate "drops." These are nothing more than pieces of acetate approximately 15 by 15 inches with a small dowel rod taped to one edge, which allows them to hang vertically from the top bars of the model stage down to the stage floor. The other part is a piece of illustration board, also approximately 15 by 15 inches, which, like the acetate sheets, has a dowel rod attached to one edge. It, however, is a grid similar to

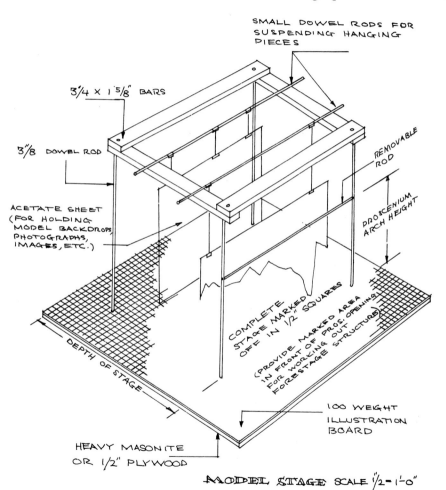

40. *Diagram of model stage unit*

SMALL DOWEL RODS FOR
SUSPENDING HANGING
PIECES

3/4 x 1 5/8" BARS

3/8 DOWEL ROD

REMOVABLE
ROD

PROSCENIUM
ARCH HEIGHT

ACETATE SHEET
(FOR HOLDING
MODEL BACKDROPS,
PHOTOGRAPHS,
IMAGES, ETC.)

COMPLETE
STAGE MARKED
OFF IN 1/2" SQUARES

(PROVIDE MARKED AREA
IN FRONT OF PROS. OPENING
FOR WORKING OUT
FORESTAGE STRUCTURE)

DEPTH OF STAGE

100 WEIGHT
ILLUSTRATION
BOARD

HEAVY MASONITE
OR 1/2" PLYWOOD

MODEL STAGE SCALE 1/2"=1'-0"

41. *Theatre Projects model theater*

the stage floor and in the same scale. To use these two parts, simply tape any selected image or images onto the acetate sheets in whatever pattern is desired and hang from the crossbars over the floor grid. (It is also possible to draw a grid directly on an acetate drop, provided acetate inks are used. This grid can also be used over backdrop drawings.) When the desired visual effect is obtained, drop the grid piece behind the acetate one; placement of the image can then be read in scale. Precise measurements are obtainable in this manner as to the image's height from the floor plane; its distance from center line and from curtain line can be read by noting where the vertical grid touches the floor grid. Figure 42 should clear up any questions concerning the use of this helpful adjunct to the model stage structure. In figure 43, the treetop forms are secured to acetate drops similar to the ones just described.

It is also a relatively simple matter (as shown in fig. 44) to make a model turntable (*A*) which, as in the full-scale stage plant, is usually built into the stage floor as a permanent feature of a particular theater. The revolving mechanism of the stage floor grid was obtained at a local discount store and is nothing more than a plastic kitchen-cabinet, ball-bearing lazy-susan unit (*B*). These come in at least two sizes. The small outer ridges of the tops of these units allow the placing of illustration board circles inside which can be secured with acetate glue. And if you really want to

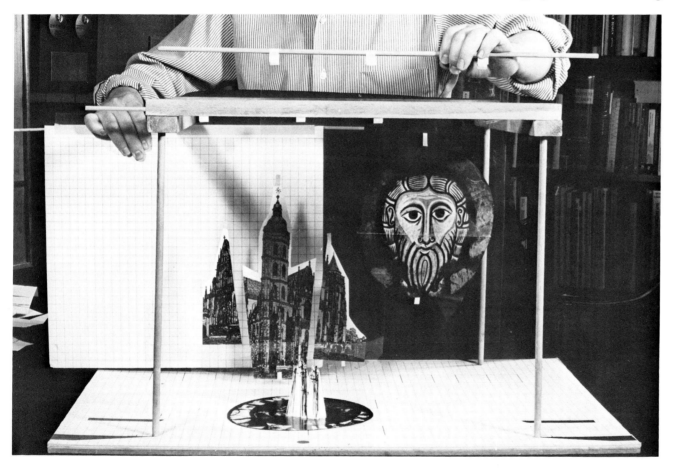

43. *Scenographic model:* As
    You Like It

take the time—or incur the expense—small motors from hobby equipment manufacturers are available; although a waste of both time and money, for some the magic of pushing electronic buttons makes the investment worthwhile.

NOTE: See part 3, sections 10 and 11, for additional discussion of found images for use in the scenographic model.

6. Recording Initial Ideas

Drawing and Quick Sketches

While it is not possible to detail a complete step-by-step outline of the scenographer's work pattern in modelmaking, there are certain features of this pattern which could be expected to be similar for most scenographers, and the first of these steps most probably would be some form of graphic note making.

All scenographers must be able to draw. Most designers, in fact, cannot think without pen or pencil. Almost all certainly precede even the crudest three-dimensional structure with graphic work of some sort. Usually these drawings are not meant for the eyes of any but the scenographer himself; they are nothing much more than a visual shorthand which he alone can later interpret. The character and number of these

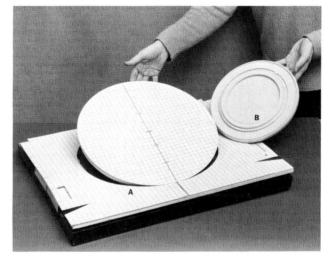

44. *Model revolving stage unit.* A, *turntable;* B, *lazy susan*

drawings, moreover, vary greatly with individual scenographers. Therefore, in the very first encounters with an idea, the scenographer needs materials and techniques which will allow him to record his idea in the most expeditious manner. Over a period of time, most scenographers develop strong affinities for those tools and methods which allow him to express his ideas in the most immediate way. It should always be kept in mind that drawing has distinctly different purposes at the various stages of the design process.

At a later time the scenographer will probably make more elaborate sketches to supplement the model. For now, however, we are concerned only with the very first drawings the scenographer makes—the initial idea expressed in its most elemental form—and then only as a step toward the construction of a scenographic model. The tools and materials for this work are relatively simple and inexpensive:

1. Pencils. While most draftsmen prefer H leads (2H, 3H, for example) for drafting, B leads, which are softer and darker, are better suited for sketching. Colored pencils can at times suggest qualities not possible with black lead alone.

2. Pen and ink. The various mechanical pens now available which use india ink, such as Rapidiograph, are favorite sketching tools for many designers. Since the points are numbered and interchangeable, a scenographer can select the quality of line that best suits his needs or temperament. The simple inexpensive crow-quill pen also retains a certain amount of popularity.

3. The felt-tip pen. This type of pen has become a very popular tool for many scenographers. Its relatively low cost plus the range of colors and tips available make it an attractive tool for sketching. Another advantage it possesses is the receptiveness of most felt-tip lines to brush and water: a line drawing such as the one shown in figure 45 can, when water is applied, become a quick, monochromatic watercolor sketch with atmospheric qualities not found in line drawings (fig. 46).

It should be kept in mind, however, that drawings which are diagrammatic in nature are of more value to the scenographer whose intent is to make a three-dimensional structure. These drawings, unlike most scenic sketches, stress the placement of solid forms in space rather than the flat pictorial qualities of the finished-set drawing. Figure 47, therefore, with its higher vanishing point, shows a truer approximation of the setting's depth; this type of drawing better serves the scenographer than figure 48, which does not show much floor space at all.

In fact, a drawing such as the isometric sketch shown in figure 49, which shows no perspective at all, is probably more useful as a step in the modelmaking process than those drawings which are more concerned with pictorial compositional values. Here real space is easier to see and comprehend than in any sketch in perspective. It would be well to keep in mind Adolphe Appia's advice to a student of design to "design with your legs, not with your eyes."

4. Conte crayon. The Conte crayon—both black and red—has long been a favorite sketching tool for designers: Its value, however, lies in its ability to give atmospheric qualities—the play of light and shadow—quickly. It is less useful to the scenographer whose primary purpose is determining the constitutent forms of a model.

46. *Felt-tip drawing (after water application)*

HORIZON LINE

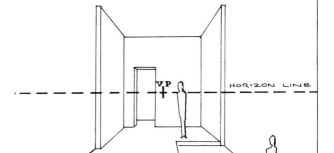

HORIZON LINE

47. Line drawing emphasizing spatial qualities

48. Line drawing emphasizing pictorial qualities

5. Layout pad. Usually a sketch goes through a series of modifications; the nature of the layout paper is that, unlike tracing paper, it has body enough to withstand pen and ink or a limited amount of watercolor but, unlike most other types of paper, is transparent enough to make tracing of images feasible.

Preliminary Paper Structures

Quite often preliminary three-dimensional work and rough sketching go hand in hand. And, while it is not uncommon for a scenographer to begin explora-

tion of a possibility directly on the model stage—manipulating forms and materials in a creatively undirected form of play—almost all do make rough drawings of an idea or of an isolated unit of scenery beforehand. Most often the process follows a line of development such as the one indicated in figure 50. Here the sketch (*A*) helps determine a basic intention. This drawing is less useful, however, than the crude paper structure which is made after it, which, incidentally, has drawing on it to indicate features which in the final structure will be three-dimensional (*B*). While the final unit (*C*) certainly had its inception in

49. *Isometric drawing of setting*

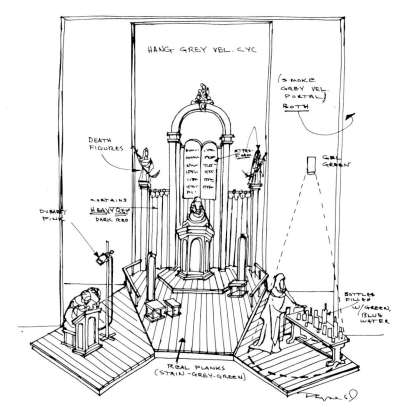

the sketch, it was the paper structure which allowed the scenographer to make the real decisions as to its scale, size, and actual form.

Working directly with paper and scissors, the scenographer is much like a sculptor who, although he may have a general idea or plan in mind, allows an idea to evolve progressively and naturally; in fact, there are times the material itself should be allowed to play a role in determining what the final form will be. (This should be an especial consideration of the scenographer who uses in his final setting newer materials, not simulations made with the traditional wood, canvas, and paint of past stagecraft procedures.) Even though these experimental forms may at a later time be made out of heavier, stronger materials, those used at this stage should be capable of easy manipulation; heavyweight paper (such as bristol board) is best suited for this work.

It must also be kept in mind that anything put on the model stage unit is automatically in a known scale. (If the model stage is ½ inch equals 1 foot, then any object placed on it becomes that scale.) A scenographer can, therefore, pretty much forget for the time the whole business of measurements and work for the satisfaction of his eye; that is, he can cut, assemble, and move the forms around the grid floor of the model unit until it "looks right." After this, he can measure the pieces, adjust them, if necessary, to the modular requirements of the materials used in building the actual scenery in the shop.

Of course, a scenographer's visual desires are always subject to the practical requirements of the scene; sight lines must be checked and the movement possibilities of the performers assured. And it should always be remembered that, even at this early experimental stage of work, the search for an exciting design should not supersede the requirements of the performers nor restrict their necessary patterns of movement merely for the sake of scenic effect. It is a wise precaution, then, even during this early period of work to keep on the model stage, along with the experimental forms being tested, a scaled figure of the human being. The scenographer must constantly remind himself of the relativity of any design to this human form.

Paper structures can be especially helpful when transferring actual research materials into a design. It is not often, however, that the forms the scenographer finds in real life will transfer directly to the stage without extensive reworking of the original construction and scale. For instance, Eugène Atget's photograph of Parisian rooftops (fig. 51) provides good factual information which could be useful to a scenographer working on the first act of Puccini's *La Bohème*, a setting whose exterior might well resemble the view recorded by Atget. But the scenographer would almost certainly have to alter both the scale and architectural features of the original to suit his own needs. The complexity of planes and forms in the Atget photograph almost necessitates that the scenographer cut and shape this information in three-dimensional form immediately rather than sketching it out as a picture beforehand. Bristol board, as we have already noted, is the best material for this stage of work (fig. 52). Eventually these rooftop forms must be given a more definite form and scale in addition to being integrated into the other requirements of the setting—the interior of the attic garret which the rooftop forms surround (fig. 53).

Finished Paper Models

Just as rough sketches are refined so that the information they contain may be made more clear, so do rough paper structures give way to more carefully made ones. The paper model, however can be either a step in making a more elaborate exhibition model or it can be complete in itself. Although extremely perishable, some paper models have been preserved in theater collections and museums. The La Scala Opera Museum has a number of these and figure 54 shows how intricately detailed some of these paper structures were. The exigencies of the working theater, however, often make it impossible for the sce-

51. Roofs in Paris, *photograph by Eugène Atget. Courtesy of the Museum of Modern Art, New York. Abbott-Levy Collection. Partial gift of Shirley C. Burden*

52. *Preliminary bristol board structures*

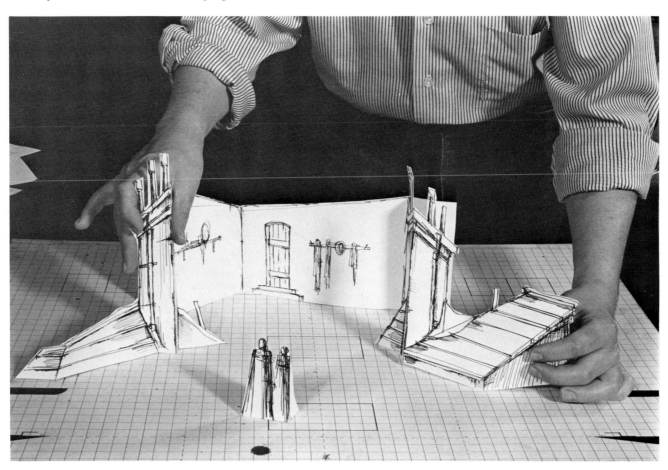

54. *Eighteenth-century paper scenographic model*

55. *Twentieth-century paper scenographic model for* Monolog O Brakie

nographer to create the time-consuming exhibition model and so, in many instances, the paper model is more than adequate to convey his intentions to those needing the information a three-dimensional representation of a design gives.

Figure 55 shows a rather unique model in which the very nature of paper is made the basis of the design; in the production of this design the quality of the paper's thinness was preserved.

In making finished paper models, there are some techniques and practices that differ from those in making the heavier models which employ other materials besides paper—balsa wood, illustration board,

wire, etc. Some of these differences in working procedure can be listed as follows:

1. As with the rough paper structures, bristol board (which is really a heavyweight paper stock) is the best material for paper models.

2. Paper models (fig. 56) can be drafted all in one piece (*A*). The thinness of the material used in these models—unlike heavier materials used in working or exhibition models —allows the bending of joints in directions not possible with illustration board; in the heavier models, thickness or material, just as with a ¾-inch thickness of an actual flat, must be taken into

account and compensated for. It is a common practice, also, to draft onto the more elaborate paper model details which eventually will be three-dimensional on the actual setting (or on the final model, if one is to be made). The floor plane of all paper models should be of a heavier stock than the walls and other pieces in it.

3. Paper models (fig. 56), unlike other types of model structures, are held to the floor plane with tabs (B). Rubber cement is probably the best glue for assemblage of paper models; unlike almost all other adhesives, it will not cause warpage in the paper. It is also possible to relocate glued units without damage to the paper. Excessive rubber cement is easily removed from the model when the project is completed.

4. Cutting the drafted model pattern can be done either with an X-acto knife or, with a reasonable amount of care, paper scissors.

5. The Ozalid process is the one most designers use for duplication of working drawings. For this process it is possible to obtain a heavy paper which can duplicate the scenographer's flat schedule directly onto a stock suitable for a paper model. This means that the same drawing which serves the shop as a working drawing for flat units can also be used to make a working paper model without the additional drafting involved when bristol board is employed. Television designers often take advantage of this timesaving step.

56. Finished paper scenographic models

This paper is also sturdy enough to take watercolor or designer's colors; so, with the execution of one drawing, it is possible to get a shop construction drawing, a paper model, and the outline for a paint schedule.

7. Procedures and Techniques of Scenographic Model Construction

Cutting Materials

NOTE: Although there are many dozens of different blades and a number of different kinds of blade holders available to model builders, eventually the individual worker will select from that great number those most congenial to his own style of working. I have, therefore, given in this text those cutting and carving instruments which I have found best serve my own approach to this craft. Through trial and error these recommendations have proved useful in scenographer modelmaking. Most of the examples shown in this book were accomplished with the cutting tools shown in figure 57.

In cutting any material, two important considerations should be kept in mind: safety and accuracy. Actually, the two go hand in hand. In cutting flat materials, such as illustration board of flat balsa woods,

the attitude of the scenographer should be similar to that of the surgeon: the right tool is necessary and rarely is the cut made all at once. Usually the first cut of the knife is made to score the material, to form a track for the later deeper cuts. Some other important practices to be observed are these:

1. Always have another piece of material under that being cut. This underpiece should be thick enough to prevent the blade going through it and scarring the surface below.

2. Always use a steel edge to guide the blade. Any other tool, such as a T square or triangle, will result in damaging both the tool and quite possibly the cutter.

3. Don't try using the same blade too long; while a new blade is extremely dangerous, a dull one can be equally hazardous. The slim-barreled X-acto knife with a No. 11 blade is probably the best all-round cutting tool for boards and small pieces of wood or plastic. Its shape and size also make it an efficient tool for most carving necessary on the model.

4. For initial scoring cuts, keep the blade as close to vertical as possible. As the cutting process continues and the blade cuts deeper, more of an angle is necessary. Once again: make all cuts in progressive stages.

5. For thinner boards and papers—such as bristol board—the X-acto knife can be used but a good pair of paper shears works just as well.

6. Wire cutters are necessary for metal wires of small

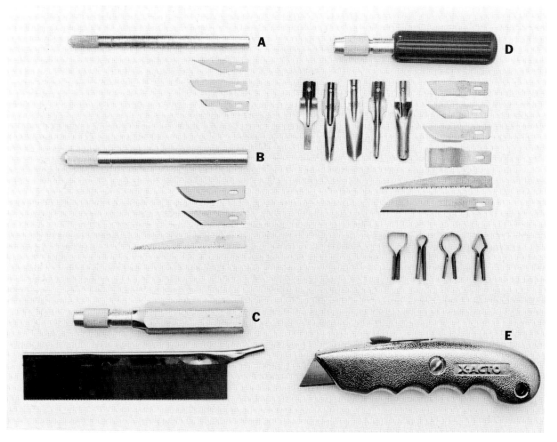

57. *Hand cutting tools.*
   A, *X-acto slim barrel knife;*
   B, *X-acto thick barrel knife;*
   C, *X-acto razor saw;*
   D, *X-acto wood carving set;*
   E, *X-acto utility knife*

diameters. Wire meshes need either small tin snips, wire cutters, or heavy duty scissors. Metal rods can be cut best with a small triangular rat-tail file. (See figure 18 for illustrations of these tools.)

7. Small pieces of balsa can be cut with the X-acto knife, but for heavier balsa pieces, the razor saw, also an X-acto Company product, is recommended (fig. 57).

8. For heavy-duty cutting jobs, special tools (fig. 58) are necessary. For cutting plastic materials, an X-acto hot knife is highly recommended (*A*). This tool also doubles as a soldering iron when the blade used to cut plastic is changed to a soldering tip. For metal materials, a jeweler's saw—also an X-acto product—is advisable (*B*). A rather expensive piece of equipment—and one which would probably not be purchased until after the scenographer goes into professional practice—is the Dremel scroll saw (*C*). This tool can save much time with cutting large, thick pieces of balsa or other harder kinds of wood. An added advantage is a side shaft which allows the attachment of either a sanding disk or a flexible-line Dremel drill. For carving small intricate pieces of furniture, sculpture, etc., the X-acto wood-carving tool kit (the smallest kit is recommended) can be a wise investment (fig. 57*D*).

9. Cutting circles in board materials can be a problem; circle cutters in figure 59 are two X-acto instruments which go far to aid in the production of good

circular cuts. Great care must still be used, however, to assure a true circle cut; some practice is necessary before uniform results occur.

10. When straight-line cuts are used in preparing floor pieces which attempt to stimulate tiles, planks, stone pieces, etc., the best practice is not to cut each of the component parts separately and then glue them to another board but to cut the desired pattern into a single thickness of 100-weight illustration board in the manner demonstrated in figure 60. The cuts shown there go only halfway through the material. In order to create a desired pattern, such as the planks being cut in the illustration, it is necessary to make two parallel cuts and then to remove the small piece between the lines. This cut should then be sanded out with the edge of a small piece of fine sandpaper folded several times to form a narrow but stiff abrasive edge (*A*).

11. An effective tool for making small holes in relatively soft materials (no harder than ordinary balsa wood) is the small battery-powered drill similar to the one shown in figure 61. These tools also come with other bits which can be used in carving, routing, or sanding. While they are limited in power, they are useful pieces of equipment and worth the small initial investment. At the first financial opportunity, however, the model builder should seriously consider buying an electric Dremel drill as shown in figure 62 (*A*). This tool, naturally, provides a much stronger

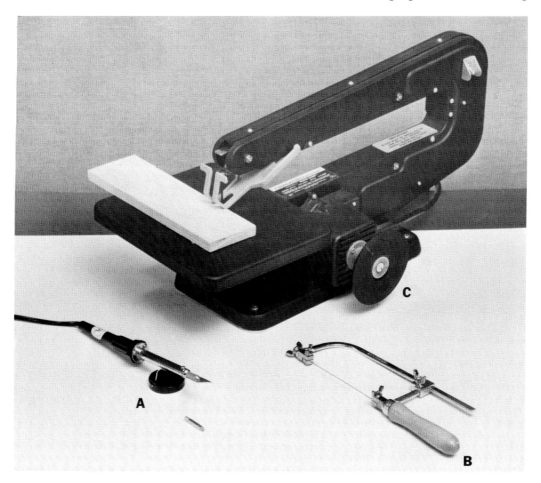

58. *Specialized cutting tools.* A, *X-acto hot knife and soldering iron;* B, *jeweler's saw;* C, *Dremel scroll saw*

59. *Circle-cutting tools. A, for cutting circles 7–15 inches; B, for cutting circles 2–7 inches*

60. *Cutting illustration board into patterns*

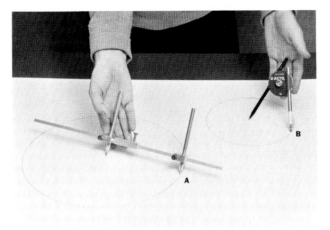

drilling power and can be used on materials that the battery-powered drill could not penetrate. It is also possible to purchase a stand for this drill which turns the hand tool into a miniature drill press (*B*). Both the drill and the stand are highly recommended.

Joining Materials and Assembly Techniques

A great deal of care and thought must be exercised in assembling the various parts of the model; bonding is extremely important. Yet there is no one bonding material suitable for all operations. Some of the more common materials and procedures are listed as follows:

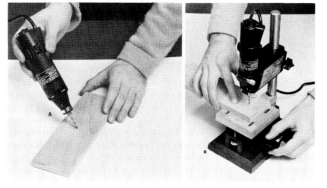

61. *Battery-powered drill*

62. A, *Dremel Moto-Tool;* B, *drill press for Moto-Tool*

Bonding paper to paper or paper to paper boards. Rubber cement is best for this purpose. It does not wrinkle when light papers are attached to other light papers or even to heavier stock. For the various types of rubber cement bonds, follow the instructions on the container. Glues with water bases (paste, Elmer's glue, etc.) will invariably cause warpage. Never use paste, for that matter, for anything. Acetate glues can be used in certain cases, but this practice is overkill for paper and is really not satisfactory.

Bonding paper to balsa woods or metal surfaces. Acetate glues are almost a must for this type of bonding. It is, however, possible to use aerosol spray adhesives such as Scotch Spra-ment, but these should be used with care. This type of adhesive works well when applying metal foil to wood or paperboard surfaces. Follow directions on the container to the letter.

Bonding textures and three-dimensional materials to flat surfaces. In most cases, light-textured materials can be attached to surfaces with gesso or by embedding them into modeling paste; sand, string, lightweight wire meshes or strands, small twigs, etc., can all be adhered in this manner without first gluing them to the surface with other types of adhesives. Nevertheless, after they are adhered, paint over the entire surface with another coat of gesso (see fig. 67).

Bonding balsa wood to balsa wood and to other materials. For the best bond between balsa woods and heavy material such as illustration board, an acetate glue (Duco cement made by Du Pont is a good product) is almost mandatory. Many of the special glues developed by modelmaking companies and purported to be manufactured especially for wood-to-plastic or plastic-to-plastic bonds are not entirely satisfactory; in fact, they often do not hold as well as ordinary all-purpose glues such as Duco cement. Special cements for gluing Styrofoam to Styrofoam or Styrofoam to other materials are practically worthless. But since acetate glues tend to melt most foam products, any Styrofoam piece should first be entirely coated with gesso, allowed to dry, and then bonded with an acetate glue. In many cases, permanent holding pins will be necessary to give strength to a joint or bond.

For special detailed work such as window units, bars, grillwork, etc., the following pattern of work is suggested:

1. Draft the unit onto lightweight illustration board (No. 300) as shown by *A* in figure 63.

2. Cut and pin the materials to the drafted pattern with dressmaker's or modelmaker's pins (*B*, fig. 63).

3. Either put small amounts of glue over the joints or, preferably, glue each joint of the unit piece by piece, applying a little more glue over the juncture after all the work is completed. Allow the unit to dry and then remove any holding pins. Since some glue will invariably drip onto the illustration-board pattern under the joints, the unit will probably have to be carefully cut away from the board with a sharp X-acto knife using a No. 11 blade.

4. The unit will gain strength when coated with gesso.

5. For the transparent part of window units, use lightweight sheet acetate glued to the back. A very light coat of flat spray-white will allow special painting to be done on the window, such as simulating dirty glass, cracked panes, or stained glass. Rosco dyes, used for painting projection slides, is recommended for stained-glass effects.

NOTE: An inexpensive biology probe and tweezers (see fig. 18, *I* and *J*) are handy tools for placing and holding small members of an intricate unit in place. The probe is also useful for creating priming holes in tough materials (such as 100-weight illustration board)

64. *X-acto holding devices*

work is required and both hands are necessary. These units come in three variations: a single clamp, a double clamp separated by a short bar, and a double clamp with an attached magnifying glass (as *B* shows).

Applying Heavy Coatings and Textures

1. Gesso is best applied with a No. 4 or No. 6 flat red sable brush kept for that purpose only, although some scenographers prefer pointed brushes rather than flat. While it will not retain its usefulness as a painting tool, an older brush which is no longer suitable for watercolor work is still serviceable for applying gesso. It must be washed out, however, immediately after use, since gesso dries quickly. A gesso brush will last several years if carefully maintained. (All brushes should be cleaned in cold or tepid water; hot water ruins the bristles of any good brush.) When applying the gesso coat to a model, attempt to give a slight texture to the surface rather than striving for one that is completely smooth. This slightly textured surface tends to catch light in such a way as to give the model a greater illusion of solidity and will give a better idea of how the full-scale setting will appear. It is something of the same principle as applying broken painted textures and patterns—such as spattering—to flat surfaces; the effect causes these surfaces to appear more solid (fig. 65).

when permanent holding pins are required. There are two pieces of equipment—both relatively inexpensive—which can aid in the assembly and finishing of small, hard-to-hold units. Figure 64 shows both: *A*) a small vise with suction cup attachment on its foot and *B*) X-acto's Second-Hand, a device with small spring clamps to hold materials steady when delicate

2. If heavier textures are desired, other materials

can be applied to the surface of the model at the same time as the gesso. For instance, plastic sand can be introduced into the gesso as the basic coat is being applied. This is done, by first, dipping the brush into the gesso and, second, dipping the wet brush carefully into a small portion of the sand. This mixture can then be applied onto the desired surface with the results being as shown in figure 66. It is possible to build up very heavy effects in this manner. Other materials—such as string, wire, cloth, or small pieces of foam or balsa—can also be applied to the model surfaces and affixed in the same manner; for light materials the gesso will act as both a binder and covering agent. For heavier materials, however, the material should be glued to the surface beforehand and then, when the glue is set, be covered with the gesso coating. Figure 67 shows some textures possible for scenic models.

3. For even heavier textures than possible with gesso, acrylic modeling paste is necessary (C in fig. 67). This material allows the scenographer to create heavily molded forms and surfaces not attainable with gesso (fig. 68). If this material is applied too thickly, however, there is a tendency for it to form cracks as it dries. The best practice is to build up the form or surface in several successive layers, allowing each to dry adequately before the next layer is applied. Even with this precaution, though, some cracks will occur. These are fairly easily corrected, however, by filling

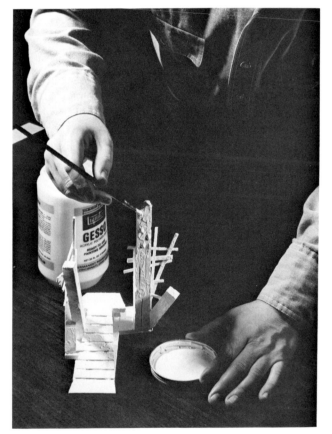

65. *Application of gesso*

66. *Sand textures on scenographic model:* Home

them with more paste when the object is completely dried. Modeling paste, unlike gesso, must be applied with tools other than brushes; oil painting knives—which come in a variety of sizes and shapes (see fig. 18, *L*)—are the best tools for this purpose. It is also advisable to have a well-defined understructure before applying the paste, so that it will be no thicker than necessary; Styrofoam is an easily worked material for creating these irregular forms. It is also a good practice, after the paste is applied, to coat the dried form with gesso which has a slightly tougher surface than modeling paste in addition to taking paint better.

It is possible to duplicate almost the exact texture specified in a model (fig. 69) in full-scale scenery (fig. 70) with a number of new materials now in use in scenery building shops. These three-dimensional textures are accomplished in the scene shop in several ways:

1. For heavy carved forms and moldings (*A* in fig. 70) sheet Styrofoam (which comes in standard sizes of 1 inch by 2 feet by 8 feet, and 2 inches by 2 feet by 8 feet, in addition to blocks of various sizes) can be easily cut and shaped with simple hand tools, heavy sandpaper, hot-wire, and hot-gun.

2. For heavy overall textures—such as plaster or stone surfaces—polyurethane foam comes in pressurized containers (allowing it to be sprayed directly onto a surface), or it can be purchased unmixed and combined in the shop so that the foam can be either

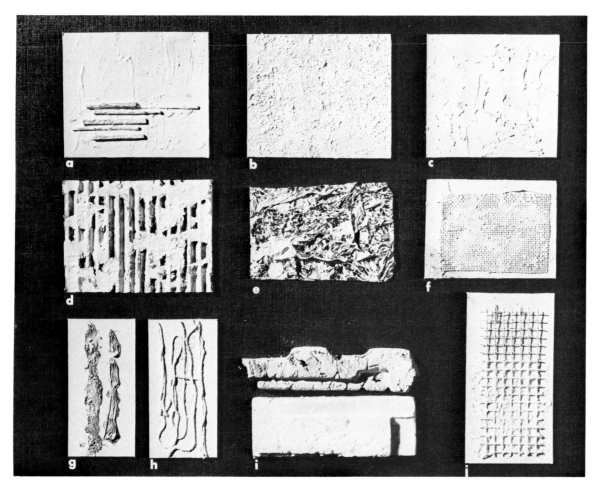

67. *Scenographic model textures.* A, *gesso on illustration board over balsa wood;* B, *gesso with plastic sand;* C, *modeling paste;* D, *gesso on corrugated board;* E, *gesso on metal foil;* F, *gesso over wire screening;* G, *liquid solder;* H, *gesso over string;* I, *gesso over Styrofoam;* J, *gesso over wire mesh*

68. *Application of modeling paste:* Cyrano de Bergerac

69. La Bohème
scenographic model

70. *Detail of setting:* La
Bohème

cast or poured. (Poured foam used to simulate piled snow is found in figure 70 [*B*].) Figure 72 shows the effect of heavily applied spray foam. (See also fig. 17.)

All these materials are lightweight, inexpensive when compared with other materials needed to obtain the same results, and take paint readily (although it is usually much easier and quicker to spray-paint these surfaces than using brushes to cover them). All foam surfaces, however, should be sealed with water-base paint before applying any acetone-based paint such as those available in aerosol cans. For additional material on using foams and plastics to achieve three-dimensional surfaces and forms, see *Designing and Painting for the Theatre* by Lynn Pecktal, chapter 10.

Force-Drying Applied Surfaces and Textures

All the materials used for model textured surfaces air-dry in a reasonable amount of time. The drying process can be, however, speeded up if necessary. Gesso, for instance, can be force-dried without unduly cracking the surface or warping the forms by putting the coated objects into a very low temperature oven with the door left open. A hand-held blowing hair dryer is also useful in drying a gesso painted surface quickly. Care must be taken, though, that the drying process is not too rapid, since this would cause warpage, especially to flat surfaces painted with gesso.

This is even more true of force-drying objects or surfaces coated with modeling paste.

Finishing the Exhibition Model

The painting of an exhibition model is not very different in approach from the manner in which a scenic sketch is made. Much of the technique, if not all the materials, is similar; in both instances, however, a number of like principles operate. Perhaps it would not be time wasted to review some of those techniques and principles before going on to the finishing of the exhibition model. The three most important principles in making a scenographic sketch could be summarized as follows:

1. Build up the work in layers, from background forward.

2. The progression of the sketch should be from mass to detail. (That is, lay in the large elements of an object before superimposing the painted detail over it.)

3. Highlight the details last; deeper shadows can also be added at this time.

In other words, do not paint the sketch "by the numbers" in the manner of the painting kits available from hobby shops, where the canvas is broken into a myriad of small individual shapes each with a number—the painter's task being merely to match each shape with a correspondingly numbered tube of paint.

71. Technicians pouring polyurethane foam

Most painters, in fact, count on the underlying layers of paint to give quality and depth of surface to each of the subsequent ones. Special effects both in the scenographer's studio work and in the final scene painting on the actual scenery often depend on the transparency of these various layers of paint. In its simplest form, the scenographic sketch can be outlined as follows (fig. 73):

1. Define outline on white material (*A*). (Illustration board or heavy watercolor paper is preferable to lightweight materials.) The surface of any water-

72. *Use of spray foam on scenery:* Suddenly Last Summer

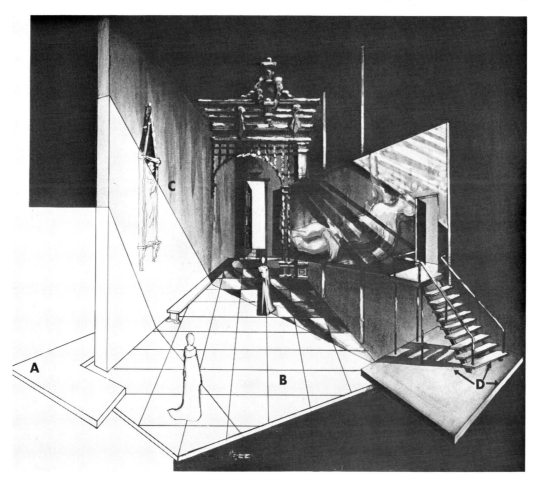

73. *Steps in making the scenographic sketch.* A, *outline of sketch in pencil or ink;* B, *build up surface transparent layers of wash or pastel;* C, *apply more detailed layers of dark and light medium;* D, *apply deepest shadows and brightest highlights last*

color material is very important; it should not be too slick—such as the almost glossy surface found on hot-press illustration board—or too highly textured. Most scenographers over a period of time develop an affinity to one type of paper or board over another; experimentation with various materials will reveal this preference.

2. The basic tonality (either watercolor or pastel can be used) is laid over the entire outline (B). In any technique used, certain large effects can be created at this stage. In the drawings of Robert Edmond Jones, the direction of the Conte crayon is clearly visible in the final sketch; in this preliminary stage, he allowed this basic coat to provide much of the texture and form of the finished work. In any case, it is always desirable to let some of this background show through the overlaying coats of paint, not attempt to cover it up entirely. It is also possible to define planes and objects simply with line and minimum shading; again, practically all Robert Edmond Jones's work demonstrates the value of this technique.

3. Large masses (plus their shadows) are laid over the background usually in dark colors and with a minimum of detail differentiation (C and D).

4. Details are placed at appropriate points on the dark masses. (In most cases these details are also the highest areas and would be where the light catches on the form.)

5. Shading can then be reinforced and final highlighting added at the end.

6. It is advisable to give the entire finished rendering a light spray with a nonglossy plastic spray (workable fixative is recommended) to seal and protect the surface.

Figure 74 shows the front view of a model based on the same design we have just been examining in the scenic sketch. Again, as we have already pointed out, the finishing of this exhibition model follows approximately the same steps as when making the scenic sketch.

All the principles apparent in figure 73 can be directly applied to the finishing of the scenographic model: most important, neither should be done piecemeal but in successive layers. Figure 75 shows more clearly the following elements of the finished scenographic model:

1. Unfinished model materials (illustration board, balsa wood, etc).

2. Texture coat consisting of modeling paste which has also been given a coat of gesso. (For lighter textures, gesso alone might be applied to the unfinished model materials; even with gesso, a slight texture is possible.)

3. Basic tonality applied with aerosol spray paint. (In this instance, a light-colored wood stain is the paint used. This, as with most wood stains, is rela-

75. *Steps in making the scenographic model*

tively transparent but tends to produce darker areas in the depressions of the texture coat. These differences in paint surfaces are often desired, since it more nearly approximates paint techniques used on actual full-scale scenery.)

4. Other coats of darker aerosol sprays are very lightly added to this basic color to produce a deeper and more varied tonality. The objective, as with the scenic sketch, is not to cover completely the surface with each successive coat but to build up a richer surface with more depth and luminosity than is possible with a single coat of opaque spray. Most of the aerosol paints and stains have a slightly glossy finish which tends to give a more lively surface to the complete model.

5. The model can now be more deeply shaded and articulated with brushwork and inks. Sepia ink is a good shading color if the effect of age is desired. Age tends to turn surfaces of materials brown; if the shading is done with washes of india ink, the effect is often that of dirt, not the passage of time. In some instances, of course, dirt is the effect desired, but in most instances, the browner, more transparent tonality provided by sepia is preferable to that of india ink. In figure 76, the following possibilities are apparent:

6. Found images may be incorporated (which could also be incorporated into a scenic sketch) into the model. Quite often this image gives the scenographer

his key to the basic tonality he desires; but it is also possible for him to tone the image with inks or watercolor. Images should be securely glued to heavier board with rubber cement when made part of a model.

7. Metallic members of the model can be left with their own color and surface unfinished; however, metal often needs a protective coating of plastic to keep it from tarnishing.

8. Final highlighting and enrichment of highly textured surfaces can be accomplished with water-soluble or acrylic metallic colors now available to scenographers. Metallic pastes can also be used for the same purpose.

Backgrounds for the Scenographic Model

The background for the model can serve two functions at once; it will, of course, be part of the model itself, but, if not permanently attached to the model floor plan, can also be used as a painter's paint schedule. It is even possible to photograph this background for use as a slide projection or it can be duplicated onto a scenic unit in the manner discussed in part 3, section 12 (see "Use of Photographic Images in Full-Scale Scenic Painting"). If used as the basis for painting a backdrop, an acetate sheet which has been inked into a half-inch grid will be necessary for the painter in order to reproduce the drop in full scale. The ace-

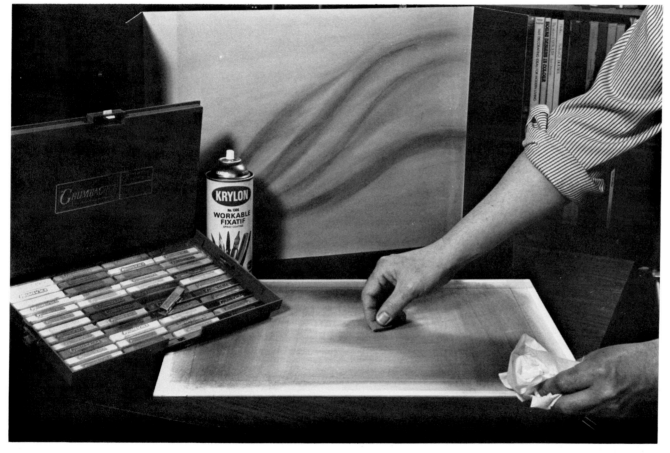

tate grid described above in section 5 can be used for this purpose. The background can be made in several ways; two possibilities are as follows:

1. Flat pastel and watercolor renderings (fig. 77). Pastel is the best material for obtaining atmospheric effects. (These effects can be duplicated on the stage either by a lens projector or by a Linnebach projector which requires no lens; the Linnebach is actually superior in some ways for soft-edged images, although brightness is often a serious drawback in its use.)

2. Found images (fig. 78) can be assembled onto an illustration-board backing (*A*). If a more uniform tonality is desired, the images can be "brought together" with inks, watercolors, etc. (*B*). The results, as with the background described above, can be reproduced in full scale by similar techniques used with any other flat design.

Set Decoration for the Scenographic Model

This area of modelmaking is often the most troublesome for the scenographer; the various items which comprise it are usually small in scale yet require great care in execution in order to give the desired finish to the model. On the actual stage, one would rarely be called upon to put crude kitchen chairs into a palace throne room; yet this is often the effect one sees in a model. The larger forms and surfaces project one feeling, the set decoration gives another. And while it is possible to obtain miniature furniture and set properties, sometimes in an actual period, they are rarely compatible with the scale used in the model and often extremely expensive. These items, therefore, must almost always be fabricated by the scenographer if a totality of effect is to be obtained. Let us examine some of the problems in set decoration of the model in more detail.

Furniture and Other Set Dressings

Most furniture for model settings (fig. 79) must be made. It is possible, however, to obtain some miniature furniture in half-inch scale from the toy departments of most chain stores (although most is either too large or too small). But even when the proper scale is found, most of these items must be modified to correspond to the style required (*A*). Pictures, murals, etc., can usually be found in magazines in appropriate size, style, and color. Other items of decoration (statuary, chandeliers, etc.) must almost always be fabricated, although there are many decorative items—such as those sold for Christmas decorations—which can be modified for use in the model setting (*B*). Many small sculptural forms and objects can be quickly fabricated by crushing and forming aluminum foil. Two weights of foil are commonly available, but the heavier of the two is recommended. Figure 80 shows a set property to be used in the inn

79. *Set decoration*

scene from the opera *Carmen*. This item—a carcass of beef (*A*)—was formed from foil as were the other set properties (*B*) in this model. It is necessary, however, in almost all cases to give these units a coat of gesso; such a covering gives a more uniform surface and allows a variety of paint to be applied. Untreated foil will accept aerosol paints but will not allow water-based paints to be used; the gesso corrects this situation. In some instances, an understructure is advisable, especially when the object being constructed is linear or attenuated. Various weights of wire will supply such a base. Foil is often used in the scenic shops to give heavy metallic sculptural form and texture to full scale scenery. It can be very useful material to the model builder as well.

Hangings and draperies. Real fabric, no matter how sheer, will not give the same effect in the model setting as when used in the full-scale setting. It is advisable, therefore, to simulate any fabric scenic piece, such as a drape or curtain, rather than to use an actual piece of fabric. It is really no problem to duplicate color; folds and textures can be indicated either by graphic techniques or built up three-dimensionally with gesso or modeling paste. The results will be much more in keeping with the scale of the model, since more precise contours can be assured (fig. 81).

Foliage, trees, and natural forms. Trees can be easily simulated by selection of small branches from actual trees or bushes. Foliage, bushes, etc., can also be simulated from materials obtained at model supply stores or from common household materials such as cellulose sponge. Small-scale plants must almost always be constructed. Precise cutting of various flat materials is necessary to obtain a desired effect of style of plant, although at best, the result can never be better than approximate. Figure 79 shows a metal paper fastener (*C*) being cut with heavy duty shears; the simple act of cutting the thin metal material produces the curvature of the leaves, although the entire frond must be shaped when assembled with other members.

Wall and floor surfaces. Although it is possible to find existing textures and surfaces which could be incorporated into a model setting, more often than not, precise styles of wallpaper, carpeting, or floor finish must be simulated if proper scales are to be maintained.

Scale Figures for the Scenographic Model

Since visualizing one scale in another is always difficult (and this is as true for the seasoned scenographer as it is for those unaccustomed to making such leaps of vision), it is always advisable to have some constant and easily understood reference of scale. No better way of accomplishing this is to include care-

82. *Possible scale figures for scenographic models. A, photographic figures; B, found line drawings and paintings; C, pen and ink sketched figures; D, crushed foil figures; E, figures carved from balsa wood and gesso; F, figures constructed of bent wire and gesso*

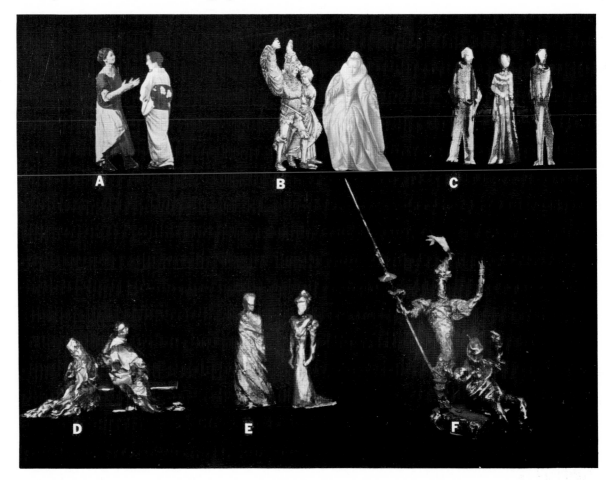

fully scaled human figures in the model. Some attention should also be paid to the style of figure used. Figure 82 shows several common ways these human representations are made; some are simply and quickly fashioned, some are small sculptures. The difference in style is really a personal matter for the model builder; he should, nevertheless, consider carefully what best complements his model. Perhaps the quickest manner by which these figures are made is to draw them on lightweight board and then cut them into the human form (C). Almost as quick, however, is the use of aluminum foil (as we have also mentioned above in the fashioning of small sculptural units) to mold these small figures. These aluminum-foil figures are especially compatible to costume works, since they tend to give a form rich in surface texture and bold in outline (fig. 83). In any case, not to consider these scale human figures along with the objects they use directly is often to miss the important focal points of a setting.

83. *Model for* Oliver *with crushed foil figures*

Part 3   *Experimental Techniques in Scenographic Modelmaking*

8. The Concept of Experimenting

Simultaneous, immediate, composite, transparent, multiple, condensed, fragmented, tangible, reconstructed—these are some of the key words. There are two others that are even more crucial: speed and space. Unexpectedly the world shrinks as it expands; there is a great deal more to see, and yet we see it faster. In trying to condense modern multiplicity into tangible form, artists have turned to certain shortcuts, to transparent, fragmented, reconstructed images where two compelling illusions—speed and space—act as basic source material. (Katharine Kuh, *Break-Up*)

Many artists of the twentieth century—painters, sculptors, printmakers, and even scenographers—have all but rejected the age-old practice of first getting a complete concept in mind and only then, using a limited number of basic materials and a restricted technique, working out that concept into a predetermined result. It is now acceptable—in fact, almost mandatory—in every art form to include techniques, materials, and approaches which would have been unthinkable even a hundred years ago; the conscious use of accidental results, the breakdown of barriers between two-dimensional and three-dimensional work, and the combination of diverse elements and mediums into a single work are now well entrenched in the common consciousness of every working artist. The reasons for these developments are many; we live in a world that mainly depends on the assembly line for most of its needs; we have instruments which allow us to view anything in the world in a quick succession of single images or in any number of superimpositions, permutations, and scales; change and chance have become important elements in both our lives and our art. All these directions have made it increasingly apparent that the art of the twentieth century is mainly one of assemblage. The bringing together of preexisting forms and images into new contexts and configurations has been and continues to be a dominant trend; painting, music, sculpture, dance, all art forms, in fact, have been greatly influenced by the artist's seeking of new meanings out of the innovative combination of both exotic and commonplace elements.

The artist, then, is no longer forced into a prescribed pattern as to the selection of his subject matter or the manner by which he expresses that subject matter. And if there has been one overall change in the attitude toward the making of art it is that the artist thinks of himself less as a creator of works springing from the deep recesses of a singular and mysterious ego and more as an expert assembler of images and forms gleaned from an objective world.   85

This more intense inspection of that objective world does not rule out the individual artist's point of view; it does, however, make the old romantic vision of the artist as a remote and incomprehensible figure less viable. Few artists today insist on the premise that the most important reason behind their work is to expose their own intensely subjective, mystical state of being. Self-expression has given way to the desire to express the world outside the single individual. This world has, the artist of today realizes, an infinitely rich store of materials and experiences to offer; his purpose is not so much to call attention to his own peculiar state of mind as it is to show to others some of that richness and diversity he in his own experience has found. This is especially true for the scenographer whose work is primarily dedicated to the service of others. As a result of this desire for an expanded vision, the creation of the static, literal picture has all but given way to the ordering of forms, objects, colors, textures, light, and time—all derived from the objective world—into a fourth-dimensional flux. The scenographer's job is no longer the making of imitative illustrations; it is nothing less than the assembly and management of images in time.

Modelmaking is unquestionably the most productive approach to solving the many complex problems of present-day scenography. Modelmaking is also, as we will see in this section, a serious form of experimentation; and the prime reason to construct any model is not simply to realize a static image in three dimensions from a two-dimensional drawing but better to understand how form, space, and the actions of the performer interrelate. As Robert Benedetti, a director who has written extensively on the relationship between director and scenographer, quite accurately points out, "Preliminary model-making should be considered as a form of 'three dimensional sketching'. Such a model should provide enough shape and indicated detail to allow for visualization, but not to such a degree of completion that making of the model becomes an end in itself. For purposes of concept development, a really useful model is one that could be accidentally sat upon without anyone minding too much." While Benedetti, as a director, makes his greatest demands of those most utilitarian aspects of a scenographic model (and to a large extent denies the usefulness of fully realized exhibition models), the basic good sense of his observations is sound. Modeling can, however, also aid in the discovery of entirely new forms and visual relationshps. A telling example as to how much experimentation opens the imagination of the artist to innovative possibilities is clearly seen in the work of the early twentieth-century Spanish architect Antonio Gaudi, who, while not a scenographer per se, did produce a number of structural principles and visual concepts which directly relate to modern scenographic practice.

When Gaudi was in the preliminary planning stages

of his masterpiece, the Church of the Sagrada Familia in Barcelona, Spain (fig. 84), he did not look back to the traditional architectural solutions of the past; nor did he base his work on accepted architectural principles—the post and lintel or any of the various arches which developed during the past two thousand years. Rather, he did nothing less than create a whole new vocabulary of shapes and forms; shapes and forms he felt best suited his own deeply held concepts as to how a twentieth-century cathedral should be constructed and experienced. Throughout the long years of research he did make numerous drawings and plans; these were, however, almost all based on the direct observation made while testing the effects of gravitational pull on linear forms and structures. Certainly his results would have been all but impossible without the large complex models (similar to those shown in figure 85) he constructed in his studios. This experimental model, along with the others he assembled, revealed to him unique architectural forms, natural shapes which had been overlooked in the long history of architectural development; moreover, the characteristic outlines of these forms could only be realized *in terms of gravity*. And it is some measure of Gaudi's individual visionary genius that all the models which led to force these forms *were actually constructed upside down*.

Like Gaudi, the scenographer working in today's theater clearly need not restrict his visions only to

84. Church of the Sagrada Familia

85. *Experimental model by Gaudi*

those tried-and-true forms accumulated throughout the history of scenery and stage machines; but modeling is, I believe, the key to achieving that freer vision.

In the following pages we will be exploring—in much the same way Gaudi approached his own special architectural problems—experimental aspects of the scenographer's art. The kinds of experimental work which will be suggested cannot, however, be entirely outlined or shown in step-by-step instructions. All that can be done is to raise a few basic (and, I hope, provocative) questions concerning the type and nature of experimental work possible when scenographic modelmaking is undertaken in the studio and to suggest some of the tools, techniques, and materials which should prove helpful in such work. The whole basis of this activity rests, however, in the concept of *creative play*. This concept merely holds that the scenographer—as with every other creative artist—must in his continuing practice allow for periods of time in which his work is not directly project-oriented (that is, being done for a specific production during a specific segment of time with a specific deadline set) but is geared only toward exploring the *random* and *chance possibilites* which present themselves to him through accidental and undirected activity. Creative play is, next to actually experimenting on a full-scale stage, the most positive and active way of increasing a scenographer's sensitivity and aware-ness to the vast potential which exists in the world outside the stage door; a world which he must never stop observing or exploring. Moreover, this is an ac-tivity not meant for student days alone; it is one which no visual artist ever outgrows. If the scenographer does not make a positive and continuing effort to ex-pand his vision through creative playful experimen-tation, he will soon be caught up in an ever-decreasing circle of past solutions, the result of which can only be an increasingly sterile imitation of his own vital work.

In the remaining part of this section four main areas of investigation will be undertaken: the role of exper-imental modelmaking in the scenographer/director relationship; the use of existing images in the sceno-graphic model; the use of found objects and materials as a basis for a scenographic model; and the various ways 35-mm projections and projection equipment can be used in the scenographer's creative work. These categories, however, used either separately or in combination, offer literally an infinite scope to the practice of scenography. (For additional information and discussion of the underlying principles and phi-losophies presented herein, please see the Bibliogra-phy.)

9. The Role of Experimental Modelmaking in the Scenographer/Director Relationship

It is to be expected that much of the scenographer's experimental work will be done independently in the studio away from the influence and interference of others. But it is equally true that much must be ac-complished in the company of other theater artists, most notably in tandem with the director of the pro-duction. A close communication is a necessity for the resolution of the many problems raised by even the simplest of productions. Before we continue our in-vestigation of experimental techniques and principles in scenographic modelmaking, it would be wise to briefly consider the nature of that relationship be-tween scenographer and director as well as to discuss how the activity of modeling can further understand-ing between the two.

In *The Empty Space*, Peter Brook says this about the basic relationships he shares with other artists in the working theater: "In performance, the relationship is actor/subject/audience. In rehearsal it is actor/subject/director. The earliest relationship is director/subject/designer."

Most directors would agree with Brook; each indi-vidual production begins its trek to the stage when these two sit down to plan the spatial and visual form of their project. Diagramatically, these discussions often take the path suggested in figure 86. Study of this outline clearly shows that while abstract discussion is integral to working out any production, there are many instances when it becomes necessary for the scenographer to show in concrete visual terms what he is actually thinking. And it is during this period of communication that both scenographer and director must come to an understanding concerning two specific areas. There are 1) the *spatial relationships* embedded in the text (not necessarily those specific stage directions written by the author), which must be prepared for and accommodated in the scenographer's floor plans; and (2) the *tonalities* also inherent in the text (and often equally hidden from the casual investigation of the uninformed reader), which give any production its particular emotional effect on an audience. Let us take these two important subjects individually to see how modeling promotes this all-important scenographer/director relationship.

The Scenographic Model in the Fashioning of Stage Space

While the forging of an understanding between the director and the scenographer can be accomplished through dialogue and graphic work (and, of course, much of it is), unlike verbal indications of size, distance, depth, or height, and unlike the illusory indications of real space on a flat surface, the scenographic model—no matter how crude its form or finish—introduces *real* space immediately into any discussion where it is used. Although it is possible to misread actual distances or sizes of spatial areas because of differing scales, the perceptions the model fosters are *always* more accurate and less deluding than those suggested by graphic work. Let us examine more closely a model used for an actual production, Ugo Betti's *Crime on Goat Island*, to see just what this form of communication can tell us that other forms of communication cannot.

It is not difficult—even at first glance—to see the effect of the scenographer's total *visual influence* on the scenic environment shown in figure 87; but this influence is easier to study in the model which preceded actual building of the setting on the stage, figure 88. What is not obviously apparent in either production photograph or model is how the scenographer and director arrived at certain configurations of objects in space. In particular, what gives the scenographer the insight to know not only what to include in this configuration but precisely what spatial relationships are immanent in the text? For almost every scenic environment is, so to speak, arrived at in reverse from life outside the theater; that is, the performers whose actions will be greatly affected by the scenographer's work often arrive only *after* the parameters of the space are defined and the physical relations of the objects within those parameters set. Just how does the scenographer know how to ensure his decisions will mesh with the work of the director and the performer? A partial answer is that, to a very great extent, we cannot avoid the observation that scenography *is* directing; nor is it unwarranted to see in the fashioning of an environment a direct link to performing. Robert Benedetti defines these close relationships more strongly yet, even going so far as to state that "it is the set—not the director—which will truly block the show. . . . Blocking is therefore best understood as the natural *manifestation of dramatic action within the configuration of a specific environment.* . . . I know that the design is correct . . . if—especially in realistic plays—I need to do *no 'blocking' at all.* The set should *express in its spacial arrangement the underlying structure of the dramatic action* and should channel the energy of the scene toward its crisis in a 'natural' way" (italics mine). These remarks are much akin to Jean Cocteau's remark that "Molière could place chairs on the stage so as they could almost speak."

Perhaps the most useful aspect of the model (fig. 88) is that it allows the director to examine very carefully—and to make physical adjustments if necessary—the most important single element to him and to his performers: the floor plane (*A*).

British scenographer John Bury has pointed out quite accurately that "in the twentieth century, the floor has become the most important single element in the design." And one of the most advantageous results of working with scenographic models from the outset

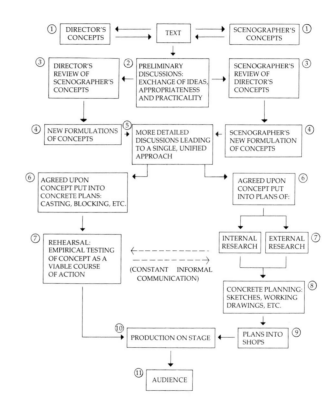

86. Chart showing director's relationship to scenographer

87. *Scene from* Crime on
Goat Island

88. *Model for* Crime on Goat Island

of discussions is that both director and scenographer are forced to concentrate primarily on this important element before they begin consideration of the more decorative pictorial elements of a design. In many cases, this concentration on the spatial demands of the production allows them to see just how little scenery is necessary to establish the sense of an environment; using graphic representations to show intent often produces the reverse: a great deal of scenery and very little consideration of the spatial requirements of the scene in question. In *The Empty Space*, Peter Brook gives these thoughts concerning this important subject:

I have often done my own designs. This can be a distinct advantage, but for a very special reason. When the director is working this way, his theoretical understanding of the play in its extension in terms of shapes and colours both evolve at the same tempo. A scene may escape the director for several weeks, one shape in the set may seem incomplete—then as he works on the set he may suddenly find the place of the scene that eludes him; as he works on the structure of the difficult scene he may suddenly glimpse its meaning in terms of stage action or a succession of colours. In work with a designer, a sympathy of tempo is what matters most. I have worked with joy with many marvellous designers—but have at times been caught in strange traps, as when the designer reaches a compelling solution too fast— so that I found myself having to accept or refuse shapes before I had sensed what shapes seemed to be immanent in the text. When I accepted the wrong shape, because I could find no logical reason for opposing the designer's conviction, I locked myself into a trap out of which the production could never evolve, and produced very bad work as a result. *I have often found that the set is the geometry of the eventual play, so that a wrong set makes many scenes impossible to play, and even destroys many possibilities for the actors.* (Italics mine)

Even in the earliest stages of a scenographer's search for images to incorporate into model experiments, he should seek out those which contain strong emphasis on floor or ground planes. (The setting for the production of David Storey's *Home* was inspired by just such an image [see figs. 33, 34].) The floor plane in some productions, such as the setting for a German production of *Troilus and Cressida* shown in figure 89 becomes, in point of fact, not only the most important scenic element but virtually the only one.

Let us now give our attention to all the influences the scenographer exercises in a production and list them in the order that the director and the scenographer are likely to discuss them (see fig. 88):

1. Floor pattern and level change (*A*).
2. Objects directly used in the action of the production (furniture, seating possibilities, set properties, personal properties [*B*]).
3. Barriers which restrict movement (although not always actual solid impediments to movement but are

treated as such by the performer), or which direct the flow of the performer's actions (C).

4. Scenic elements and objects which have a visual influence on the audience but are not direct influences on the performer or his actions (D).

There is an all-important fifth influence which does not physically alter any of the above categories but does allow for an infinite possibility of visual change: the effect of light on physical form (as indicated in the scenic drawing shown in figure 90). It is in the use of this element, moreover, that the two basic influences—physical and psychological—merge to form the condition we term *dramatic*. But since the lighting of a production cannot be adequately predicted by use of scenographic models—at least not to the extent that models help in other more physical ways—in our present study we will confine out attention to only the first four of these influences.

Specifically, the use of models in an evolutionary process allows the prime concerns of both the scenographer and director to be addressed with a minimum of misunderstanding: space, form, and the opportunity to trace physically the movement of performers within an actual three-dimensional context.

But there is one other important way models serve the scenographer/director relationship; and that is in allowing for the demonstrating and discussing of one of the production's most important visual elements: the *tonality* of the work onstage.

89. *Setting for* Troilus and Cressida

Tonality

The word *tonality* is a difficult one to define completely, since it can be used in the discussion of both aural and visual art forms. Even the best dictionary will not address adequately how we have come to use this term in theater. Nevertheless, it is a valuable word which cannot be divorced from present-day scenographic practice; every theater artist needs to have this term as part of his working vocabulary. For it is the prime function of *tonality* to provide a means for presenting subjective feelings in objective terms. And it is the *tonality* of a production that reveals the intan-

90. *Effect of light on three-dimensional forms*

gible inner dramatic meanings of any stage work. Too often, however, seeking out tonalities inherent in a dramatic text or libretto becomes little more than the arbitrary selecting of colors, with little regard as to how those colors relate either to the text which engendered them or to the forms, textures, and conditions of light underwhich they will be viewed.

Perhaps a simple experiment will introduce the important difference between these two terms: *color* and *tonality*.

Take several pieces of illustration board—approximately 3 inches by 3 inches is sufficient—and create on each a different texture similar to those textures shown in figure 67: gesso, modeling paste, sand, wire mesh, paste, etc. Leave one card without any texture at all. When these cards are dry, paint every one with an identical color—red, for instance. When the color has dried, arrange all in a row on a larger piece of white board with a few inches of space around each example. Now, shine a strong light on the board from a sharp angle. Question: *Which example is red?* The answer to this simple question is not as obvious as might first appear; for although all are painted with an identical color, all—due to the variations of texture and the response of that texture to the effects of light and shadow—produce distinctly different impressions to the eye. While, in one sense, all are still *red*, in another very real sense, all examples are markedly different in quality. These differences are readily apparent to even an untrained eye; add even the smallest amounts of other colors to these examples—as is the case with almost all objects in the natural world—and it soon becomes apparent that while we may casually speak of something being "red," or "blue," or "green," what we are really attempting to identify is not single colors but the predominate visual quality of a *tonality*. In fact, in the professional theater, we very seldom deal with pure colors in the sense that they will be seen in isolation; we are rather, almost always dealing with *predominant tonalities* which may be composed of a great number of other colors in varying proportions. Even the simple experiment suggested above demonstrates that when another element is added to a single color—texture, in this case—the variations in visual response become widely divergent.

It is a highly recommended practice, therefore, in the formative stages of a proposed production, to avoid discussions of colors as if they were to be seen in isolation and to recognize from the outset that it is more important to seek out *the tonalities inherent in a text*, not the possible colors of individual objects.

A practice common among scenographers, costumers, and even some directors is to bring to the earliest meetings of a new production—long before discussion settles down to specific styles or precise size of playing areas—bits and pieces of materials and objects which possess qualities—and tonalities—these artists feel directly relate to the text but may not be specifically called for in the playwright's written instructions or dialogue: pieces of tree bark, stones or minerals, a fragment of rusted metal, or a swatch of old cloth, all found things that may provide a jumping-off point for discussion or which may even supply direct access to important themes or motives hidden in the careless banter of the work's characters. When concrete materials are present, moreover, the consideration of color is not an amorphously abstract exercise but, rather, becomes a real means to uncover the deepest wellsprings of an author's concerns. Nor is this practice just a recent development in the theater. Peter Brook relates (also in *The Empty Space*) how William Poel, almost a century ago, used a similar practice to instruct his performers as to his feelings about their characters:

One of the pioneer figures in the movement towards a renewed Shakespeare was William Poel. An actress once told me that she had worked with Poel in a production *Much Ado About Nothing* that was presented some fifty years ago for one night in some gloomy London Hall. She said that at the first rehearsal Poel arrived with a case full of scraps out of which he brought odd photographs, drawings, pictures torn out of magazines. "That's you," he said, giving her a picture of a debutante at the Royal Garden Party. To someone else it was a knight in armour, a Gainsborough portrait or else just a hat. In all simplicity, he was expressing the way he saw the play when he read it—directly, as a child does—not as a grown-up monitoring himself with notions of history and period. My friend told me that the total pre-pop-art mixture had an extraordinary homogeneity. I am sure of it. Poel was a great innovator and he clearly saw that consistency had no relation to real Shakesperian style.

In a similar fashion, Robert Edmond Jones, even as

the scenery he had designed was being finished in the scenic paint shop, attempted to influence the manner in which the craftsmen worked. Jo Mielziner relates just how important Jones considered having bits and pieces of materials or items which evoked thoughts and feelings in those performing the most prosaic mechanical physical labor on the production:

> I recall the time when Jones was supervising the execution of the stage setting for the seventeenth-century Spanish room in *The Buccaneer*. A week earlier he had completed his design, and on this particular day the crew of fine scenic artists in Bergman's Studio was executing the set on the paint-frame below Jones's studio. Bobby couldn't bear the idea that they would think of their work as simply the job of executing a large painting; so he scurried out with me to gather up bits and pieces of what he called "living things" which related to the setting: a lovely antique bench of the period with the patina of age and the beauty of line that he loved so much; a swatch of antique yellow satin, with some black lace and a huge artificial red flower; a yard or two of heavy gold lace; one lovely Spanish Renaissance tile. These things he placed on the floor beside the setting on which the painters were at work, because Jones wanted—for himself and for all who were working with him—to be conscious of the relations of this painting to its final achievement and appearance on the stage.

But while found objects and evocative materials can begin the process of exploration for tonalities appropriate to a specific production, it is a rare instance when the scenographer's search ends by simply copying directly on the stage the outward features or dominant qualities these objects and materials exhibit. They are, rather, catalytic agents which direct attention to a more important stage of research: the seeking out in the text of the dramatic reasons why these things drew attention to themselves in the first place. This step almost invariably leads us into that all-but-inaccessible realm of the playwright's world of past experience, present concerns, and submerged motives. And it is here that one may begin to find objective clues that will lead to the understanding of why a certain tonality or range of tonalities suits a certain work. This process is time-consuming and often beset with false clues, unsuccessful digressions, and heated debate. It is even possible (almost certain) that the inherent qualities of a play were not consciously considered by the playwright himself. It is highly doubtful that Shakespeare—albeit a genius of the highest order—could have been aware of *all* of the implications of his writing and would quite probably have been amazed how rich and complex the worlds he created really are. Nevertheless, the actual process of selecting the tonalities which best suit a particular work is not as mysterious or as difficult a task as might first appear.

Read, for example, the opening scenes of *Hamlet*; then read the opening scenes of *Macbeth*. Both plays have much in common; clues abound concerning atmosphere, mood, underlying emotional currents: in both plays a sense of dread and a mood of apprehension permeate the physical characteristics of the environment in which the characters find themselves. And both plays use expressive language which summons up visual and sensory emotions in the reader: the sense of indistinct forms slowly moving in obscure light; the feeling of cold, damp surroundings; and an awareness that we are no longer in the safe world of normal human activity. These are perceptions common to both works; and yet, upon closer study, each place presents to the imagination a distinctly different locale. The world of *Hamlet* is ringed with icy-cold stone walls; the world of *Macbeth* is a plane of scrubby bush obscured by patches of dun-colored fog; the world of *Hamlet* is a deep-midnight haunt of restless ghosts straying from unquiet graves; the world of *Macbeth*, a sunless twilight settling over a blood-soaked moor where withered old women plunder dead soldiers. Both worlds are dark places filled with indistinct light and deep shadow; but— and this is important to note—they are each dramatically distinct one from the other. How can one, then, speak simply of *color* in worlds so devoid of clear and distinct choices? It is, however, possible to discuss precisely the differences between the two once we have adopted the terminology of *tonality*, especially when these discussions are accomplished by actual things which embody that which the playwright's

words stirred in our imagination but which we could not otherwise name in terms of color or describe adequately in our own abstract words. Most important of all, these discussions are quite possibly the most crucial ones the scenographer and director ever have since they literally set the *tone* of the entire production.

But is the selection of a production's tonality purely an arbitrary one; does the scenographer have the right to select only those tonalities which please his particular esthetic sensibilities? It is clearly evident that experienced scenographers do have predilections for certain forms, colors, and textures, which result in repeated tonalities production after production (and it is quite possible to detect those personal signatures in any mature visual artist); but it is also very much part of the scenographer's professional commitment to find those tonalities which convince the director that they are indeed the most appropriate ones for the particular production in question. Of course, these perceptions—even mutually arrived at—are still personal and subjective. While discussion and debate will produce areas of mutual agreement (I doubt if anyone could read the opening scene of *Hamlet* and believe it takes place at high noon on a summer day), there are also apt to be significant differences of opinion in matters of detail: If dark, how dark? If cold, how cold? If foggy, how foggy? And so on. It is wise, therefore, to have a more precise mechanism available to the scenographer and director by which primary impressions agreed upon can be made quickly objective. For I have found throughout a long history of such discussions that verbal descriptions of colors and tonalities—while they may begin the process of agreement—have a limited (and quickly reached) value in the real world of scenographic planning: when I speak of *red*, I can be assured without exception that my correspondent is "seeing" a different color than that I hold in my own mind's eye. Catsup, fire, and a bottle of burgundy held before a candle are all *red*. But who would dispute that those reds are all different with vastly dissimilar emotional connotations? Even if I were to be as specific as to say that the *red* I imagine is *blood red*, a knowledgeable listener could very well inquire, "Which *blood red* did you have in mind; that of blood in the veins or that of blood in the arteries, for one is quite different in color from the other?" While few directors I have observed would be so precise, the point is really a valid one; for the human eye is remarkably able to discern minute shades of difference in light, shadow, and color, and the human mind is fully capable of responding emotionally—as I am sure it does in the theater—to these small variations.

But how does one introduce the possibility of examining a range of tonalities into early planning stages of a production? The method I have come to adopt during the past two decades is a remarkably simple one and is a process that forces the director to become

as involved as myself in the process of precise selections of color and tonality. The basis of the system is this: I assemble a great number of examples clipped from magazine illustrations, advertisements, reproductions of paintings, bits and pieces of junk mail, etc. These are small swatches of color and tonality which I select rather than mix from basic colors in the studio. The reasons why these examples are gathered in this manner are several:

1. A vast number of swatches can be assembled very quickly from even a few sources. Every magazine contains dozens of possibilities which provide a far greater range of possibilities than could be mixed up by an individual.

2. The mind (even that of an experienced artist) often changes when confronted with a number of possibilities. Attempting to mix an imagined color often tends to close off the imagination rather than to expand it; the scenographer's effort becomes too narrowly directed, too limited in the tedious activity of mixing and matching single basic colors into more complex ones. Expertise in color mixing is, of course, an important (and in the scenic shop indispensible) skill to have; no scenographer can avoid—or should attempt to avoid the mastering of color mixing. But during the early stages of exploration, it is much better to expose the mind to a wide spectrum of possibilities rather than chain it to the mechanical and restricting activity of color mixing.

3. After having assembled a great number of color

bits, I can then allow a director to participate in that important culling process which will eliminate the great number of possibilities to a manageable few. More important, I can say to a director who has indicated preferences for a certain color range, "All right—you wanted a basically red tonality for this particular scene: just which one comes closest to what you had in mind." Once he has selected from a range of reds the one he had in mind, I can then have a firm basis from which discussion can progress. Most important of all I can say, "Yes, I know now just what you mean." Or, as it often happens, I can say, "No—I don't believe that is the right tonality for this scene." Real discussion can then take place, each of us defending the appropriateness or inappropriateness of the decision made. It is often during this process that points of view change.

4. The fact that examples clipped from prexisting sources are rarely pure in tone or color gets away from thinking in abstract terms; we no longer simply say "red" or "green" and believe that a precise color is being shared with those who hear us. In many instances, these found tonalities have no exact names and exhibit subtle graduations of one color to another in a manner that cannot be described but only shown. And while it is entirely possible to duplicate these in the scenic shops or on the stage, no amount of verbal discussion would produce the same results.

The real question, then, becomes how selected tonalities find their way into the actual production process. Here again the scenographic model can be the most efficient way to bring the two most important primary considerations—space and tonality—into an integrated whole. While there are many other areas the director and the scenographer must consider and reach agreement upon, these we have just discussed are, to my mind, the most important decisions that result from the scenographer/director relationship.

10. Use of Existing Images

It is more or less conventional wisdom to think that twentieth-century artists were the inventors of works which are assembled from preexisting images, diverse materials, and applied textures. The truth of the matter is somewhat different, however; in Herta Wescher's book, *Collage* (trans. Robert E. Wolf), our attention is drawn to the following fact:

Pictures assembled from assorted materials have an ancient ancestry, and the earliest examples known are also among the refined. It seems to have been in the twelfth century that Japanese calligraphers began to copy poems on sheets pasted up from a number of irregularly shaped pieces of delicately tinted papers. The composition that resulted was then sprinkled over with flower patterns or tiny birds and stars made from gold and silver paper, and when the torn or cut edges of the papers were brushed with ink, their wavy contours presented mountains, rivers, or clouds. . . . It is certain that collage, montage and assemblages of various materials had innumerable predecessors in past centuries but only an insignificant number of these can be related in any way to what is done today. . . . Not until the twentieth century, when creative artists took to working with it, did collage become a new and valid means of expression, one which has left its mark indelibly on the art of today.

While, as Wescher points out, collage has been in the mainstream of this century's art trends from the very first, only during the past three decades has any widespread use of this technique found its way into the scenographic process. (There have been notable exceptions; still the practice of using assembled works for scenograhic purposes has definitely remained a philosophy of theatrical thought more attuned to the second half of this century than to the first.)

One of the influences which has led to an expanded use of collage lies in the increased employment of scenic projection: images made into photographic (or painted) slides which can be directly projected onto screens or forms in the theater. And a major reason for this use of projections can be directly attributed to the nature of many dramatic works written or composed today which are meant to be viewed as a series of fragmented scenes in nonlinear sequences. The juxtaposition of the incongruent text

with the illogical image has become a customary element in the theater of today. The use of collage techniques in the planning of a production has been, therefore, a natural response to this trend. For the student of scenography, this means that traditional perspective drawings of single-view images arising from the scenographer's singular imagination has become only one aspect of modern-day scenographic training. The usefulness of collage principles, however, can be suggestive in the searching out of a design solution even when we are not creating environments which are totally divorced from a rational framework; i.e., when we are seeking concepts and images for productions with more traditional approaches.

Let us take just one example to demonstrate how it is possible to bypass certain normal steps in the scenograhic process (making numerous small exploratory sketches, utilization of traditional research findings, etc.) and to fashion a design possibility directly with collage techniques. Let us assume that in approaching a traditional play from the past—*Antigone* for instance—that we wish to retain certain historical elements in the production; that we wish to include in our design both the *orchestra circle* of the fifth-century Greek theater and images from actual sites (such as those excavated by Schliemann at Troy in the 1870s) from which the legend sprang (fig. 91).

Having sought out a number of isolated images from

91. *Ancient Greek site at Troy: Grave Circle*

92. *Ancient Greek site*

93. *Ancient Greek statue*

research sources, we then, through the use of collage, experiment by combining these images into different patterns until we have found an image which satisfies the above intentions. (While scale of the individual images does not matter all that much, a certain compatibility is necessary; by compatibility we mean images which have or can be forced into roughly similar visual points of viewing. These images can be duplicated—they were in the four steps below—by the Xerox process, after which they can be cut, separated, and reassembled into the desired configuration.) The steps in the process from isolated images into unified works could be listed as follows:

1. Finding research materials which satisfy visual needs of the scenic concept and (perhaps) the historical context (figs. 92, 93).

2. Cutting, experimenting with placement, and assembling the images into the desired configuration.

3. Finished collage (fig. 94).

4. Use of collage as a basis for a scaled scenographic model (fig. 95). (The model can then be translated into working drawings.)

Collage does not always lend itself to such specific purposes as the example just demonstrated; but, as we can easily see, the principles inherent in such work can not only be valuable insofar as they allow us to pursue certain mechanical shortcuts; they can also actively suggest original interpretative approaches to many works of the past. For example, although the action of *Antigone* is set before the palace of Creon, the basic image in the collage just shown is dependent less on the flat *orchestra* of the Greek theater than it is on the grave circle shown in figure 91. What this means is that our research images suggested a *different* locale from the traditional one; that the action could be moved to the place from which Antigone, as the play begins, has just returned—the site where the body of her brother lies unburied. (The various levels which are part of the original images incorporated into the collage also suggest various possibilities for movement not possible on the usual flat surface of the *orchestra circle*.)

Very early in their career, most scenographers become aware that found images have a power to trigger the imagination in many unforeseen ways; for this reason, it is highly advisable for all who wish to make scenography a profession to begin a systematic collection of the random images which cross their path. One never knows just when these accidental acquisitions not only may become useful but may, indeed, be responsible for an actual design.

The found image often serves, then, as the basis for three-dimensional scenic units. The source of Jocelyn Herbert's figure of Christ (fig. 96) used in the John Osborne play, *Luther*, is obviously derived from Grünewald's painting of the Crucifixion (fig. 97).

This image, however, can be used in ways other than as research source material or as a single picto-

94. *Collage design for* Antigone

95. *Scenographic model from collage of* Antigone

96. *Detail of setting for* Luther

97. The Crucifixion *by Grünewald*

rial unit. It can, as shown in figures 98–100, be incorporated into a design in ways which integrate its flat rectangular form into a more dynamic arrangement:

Several things are immediately evident in this simple exercise. Perhaps the most important point to be observed, though, is that while a precise meaning cannot be ascribed to each of these variations, it is obvious that the basic perception of the image is greatly altered in each case. And while few would agree as to exact emotion or message these variations project, it is safe to say that each sends a specifically different signal to the spectator. It is a very short step from the observation of this abstract principle to a concrete application of it. This is not to say, as some basic texts in scenography tend to imply, that curved lines always mean comedy, tall vertical ones denote tragedy, and so on. Nevertheless, it is basically a sound principle that particular forms can help project more forcefully concepts that are essentially literary rather than visual. But these forms must be tailored to support very specific problems; their size and shape do not inherently carry exact meanings.

Let us take, as an example, the first scene of Shakespeare's *Richard III*. At the beginning of the play, Richard states very definitely his ambitions—to get the throne of England from his brother, Edward IV (or from anyone who happens to stand in succession to it), by any means possible. At the moment, however, Edward is still king and at the height of his power.

This relationship can be made visually evident by showing Richard standing below a large image of Edward. (The approach we are taking in this example is not a realistic one but rather a theatrical one.) By juxtaposing this image, along with Richard and perhaps the actual throne on which Edward sits, we have both the objective and the obstacle to Richard's ambition in plain view. We could present these elements on the stage in the manner shown in figure 101.

But does this really show all we want to say; is the nature of the scene in any way furthered by this arrangement? The design is a formally balanced one; in a word, it is *static*. But the play is, if nothing else, a long series of brutal confrontations, plots, and betrayals; in another word, it is *dynamic*. Even this first scene is fraught with the violent intensity that marks the rest of the play. We need, therefore, a scenic environment which will reflect and support both the active nature of the play and savage undercurrent of this scene in particular. What is required is something which visually presents Edward's initial eminence while at the same time introducing us to the dangerous directions Richard intends to pursue in his path to the throne. Using the same elements—the overscaled image and the throne—we can create another configuration which might better support the action of this particular scene (fig. 102).

Here, several important changes have been made from our first design; the image has been, to begin

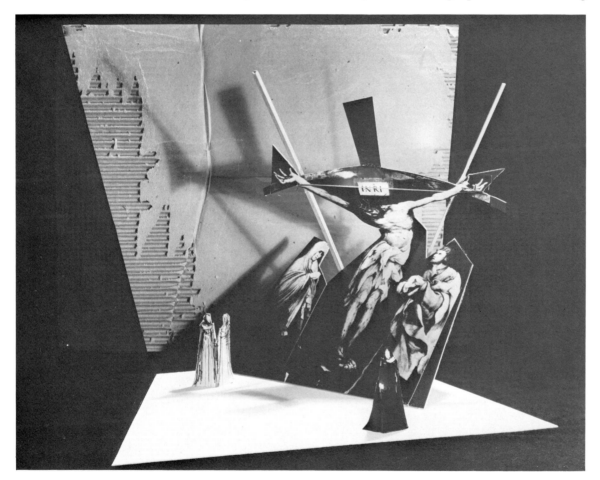

99. *Variation of same Grünewald image*

with, cut in half with a long diagonal line and separated to allow passage between the two parts. (We do, in fact, tend to read qualities of action into lines which have no other representational function; a vertical line does have a feeling of stability and order; a horizontal line is perceived to be in a state of rest; a diagonal line, such as the one imposed on the image of Edward, is the most active of the three and can be read as unstable and falling. Actually, since Richard has, at the beginning of the play, already given much thought to his ambitions, he has, in effect, already begun the process of toppling the king; that is, pushing him from the vertical toward the horizontal. In fact, the last time we see Edward he is headed for his deathbed as a direct result of Richard's plottings). It is through this broad slash, then, that the figure of Richard first emerges. Even he, according to Shakespeare's own internal evidence, is incapable of standing up straight because of his congenital deformities. And, when we first see him, the dangerously pointed form above him helps to emphasize the dangerous course he has decided for himself; a course which could, if he does not play his hand correctly, cost him not only the throne but his head. In addition, the throne is now some distance from his entrance and the way to it at an oblique angle to him, not directly in his path. Even though an audience will not immediately say to itself, "Ah, yes, I see: this design is saying to me that . . . ," it will receive information

100. Variation of same Grünewald image

101. *Design for* Richard III

103. *Still photograph from Ivan the Terrible*

that visually underscores the scene better than the first static picture; the split image of Edward becomes more vulnerable as it becomes more active, and the throne becomes an actual objective in space as well as in time.

The use of found images, either painted or projected, either in actual scale or overscaled, is likely to remain part of the scenographer's iconography for some time to come. And there are good reasons why this should be so. There are, however, some cautionary principles which should be observed in their use. Few actors, for instance, would ever consider going in front of an audience and shouting, "Hey, you out there—look at me!" And yet this is the exact effect produced in many designs using images when they were not carefully integrated into the production as a whole. In the past twenty years, many scenographers have believed themselves automatically to be modern and up-to-date by the simple inclusion of projected images into their work. The results, however, are often totally disastrous for all involved. No performer can hope to retain the attention of an audience if he and an image fifty times his size must fight for the focus. Especially in the use of greatly overscaled images, their purpose must be thoroughly considered and their effect carefully managed. A good example of how effective such images can be when integrated into the total design exists in Sergei Eisenstein's *Ivan the Terrible, Part I* (fig. 103).

It was part of Eisenstein's scenic concept to have

the characters of the drama constantly under the scrutiny of the great searching eyes of Russian iconic faces. But, it is important to note, these images always take their place in the total design; they never "upstage" the performers. They do, in fact, help us focus not so much on where a scene is taking place but what is happening in that locale. The fact that this example is taken from the cinema does not alter the principle exposed here. A less successful use of the overscaled human face was employed in a Russian production of Alexei Arbuzor's *My Poor Marat* (fig. 104). Here, the performers all but fade into the scenic background.

While these admonitions may seem to indicate an unduly cautious attitude toward the experimental use of images, the fact remains that most scenographers and directors do attempt to make sure that anything they introduce into the production "pays its way"; that no single element is allowed to distort the balance of the whole. Images can do much to further the meaning of a production, but while they may very much aid and amplify the work of a performer, and the playwright, they should never surplant it.

11. Found Objects and Materials

To a very large extent, no scenographer can avoid using in his work objects that already exist. In interior

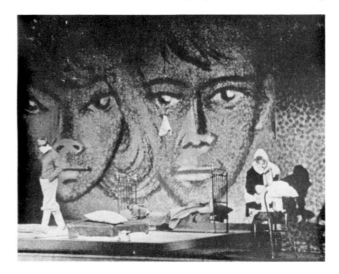

104. *Setting for Arbuzov's* My Poor Marat

settings especially, whether period or modern, he is expected to assemble appropriate items as part of the design—furniture, set properties, and set dressing. Since many of his designs deal with particular characters in a specific environment, part of his skill depends on the development of a sensitivity to the precise atmospheres that a collection of preexisting objects can evoke. Even when designing settings where furniture and set dressing have little part, he is expected to understand the visual language that results from the juxtaposition of objects and performers. For the fact of the matter is, that objects—singularly and in groups—can and do speak. The language of course, is different from that of words, but it is no less eloquent or exact than that of the actor. It is, in fact, often part of the scenographer's function to send to an audience complex and meaningful signals by the use of an object or a configuration of objects. And while these messages are not necessarily perceived by that audience on conscious levels (indeed, what is conveyed in this manner should not be an obvious statement), they can amplify an actor's role or clarify a director's point of view in situations where words would be inadequate. More importantly, they can, and very often do, enrich the play's meaning and the author's intent. Any scenographer who has worked in the theater even for a short period of time begins to see the potential of objective form in making even complicated ideas clear and meaningful. One example will suffice here:

In 1967, the National Theatre of Great Britain produced Chekhov's *Three Sisters*. It was directed by Laurence Olivier and designed by Josef Svoboda. (Pictures of this production can be seen in Richard Pilbrow's book, *Stage Lighting*, and the entire production was filmed and distributed for the 1973–74 American Theatre Film Festival). While the basic settings were not realistic, the furniture and set properties were in period; these, however, although few, were carefully considered, both as to their placement and their dramatic purpose. One set property used in the setting for acts 1 and 2 (the same locale), was given a special function to perform. This piece was an ornate clock made in the likeness of a city cathedral; a building one might expect to find in some great Russian city. Ostensibly the clock was simply a highly decorative but essentially utilitarian item; no one actually wound it, called attention to it directly, or even acknowledged its presence in the room. To the casual observer, this clock would appear to be nothing more nor less than what it was: something that most drawing rooms of the period might have had and something any scenographer decorating this setting might use. Yet, as the play progressed, this clock began to play an active part in the unfolding of the drama. It helped in a very positive way to underscore one of the underlying themes in this play; that life passes most people by; that if there is any excitement or gaiety to be had out of it, it is always in some other place. For the characters of *Three Sisters*, this better existence can only be had in a large city; in this case, Moscow. By combining the element of time (and consequently making it a constant reminder of its passage) with an image which also reminded this group of the glittering life they were missing, Svoboda created a potent symbol which made its point without intruding on the action of the play. Even the placement of the clock on the stage, set alone as it was on its own high pedestal helped to reveal the fears and obsessions of the characters who inhabit the room with it. In the film version, this image became stronger than in the stage version; at one time, the camera slowly panned across the room and came to rest on the clock. When the camera stopped, the image was out of focus; but as the chimes struck the hour, the picture cleared and gave the spectator a closeup view of this time-passing city-life symbol. There was no mistake as to the message being sent to the audience; the point was subtly but forcefully made. Objects, as we have said before, can speak; and what they say is often more eloquent and powerful than any words could ever be.

It is with this attitude in mind that the scenographer learning his craft should approach his experiments with found objects; he must look for the various ways in which he can combine abstract concepts with concrete forms, colors, and textures. He is not simply charged with the decoration of the stage space, he should think of his profession as one where the poetic and dramatic values of a production are transmitted in large part by his manipulation of elements taken from the objective world. The scenographer should also be in constant touch with the work being done in other arts. Much of the work being done there can have a significant influence on his own. Constructions, such as Edward Keinholz's assemblage and mixed media work at the Whitney Museum of American Art show how powerful statements can be composed of essentially simple elements (fig. 105). This type of construction is not unlike those which

the scenographer is required to make; the student of scenography can learn much by keeping abreast of the work of such artists as Keinholz who use the commonplace and familiar to create evocative and meaningful configurations.

Modelmakers in particular should be familiar with the work of one of America's most important artists of the past four decades, Joseph Cornell. He was an extremely sensitive artist who created a sizeable body of work from a wide variety of simple forms and materials. His work is closely related to the type of experimentation that is being suggested here (fig. 106).

The natural tendency for most scenographers is to collect: images, objects, materials—everything, in fact, that has tactile or visual interest has a peculiar fascination for those who make their living exploring the possibilities and potentials of the physical world. This is a necessary quality that all scenographers should have to a great degree, and one that must be fostered continually. It is wise, therefore, in the scenographer's student days to begin to make provision for ways to keep this ever-growing multifaceted collection vital and constantly available. A good principle to foster in this: never come back to your studio without bringing something with you; perhaps an interesting twig or a piece of rusted metal. Nobody outside the profession will ever quite understand (except those in other visual arts); but then, that is one of the reasons they are not scenographers.

105. *Assemblage by Edward Keinholz:* The Wait. *Courtesy of the Collection of the Whitney Museum of American Art, New York. Geoffrey Clements Photography, Staten Island*

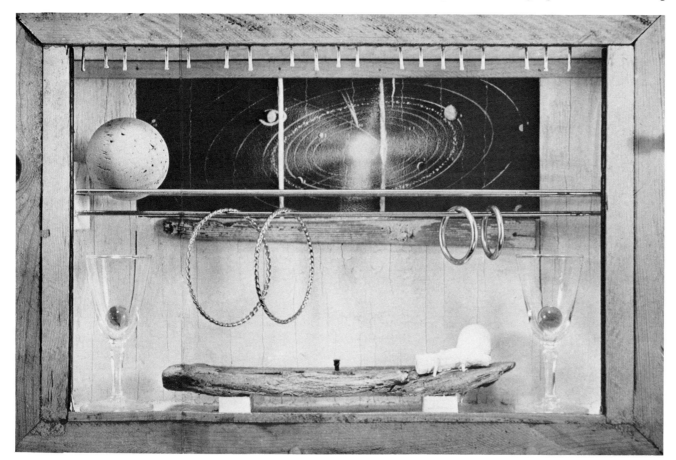

106. *Assemblage by Joseph Cornell:* Sun Box. *Courtesy of Alvin S. Lane*

It is impossible to suggest further just what the scenographer should collect or how he might go about using those things he does; notwithstanding the wide range of possible materials that present themselves to his attention every day, certain preferences will always come to the fore, both as to the nature of the material and its arrangement on the model stage. Some scenographers are partial to organic form and will always emphasize it in their work, while others will lean toward the architectonic; what they find and how they use it will probably continue to reflect these predispositions. But there is no better way to break old engrained habits and prejudices than by removing the necessity of having to put to formal use the results of these experiments. If the scenographer is not under the pressure of having to devise a design for an actual proposed production, he is apt to be more open to change and adventurous in testing new visual ideas. All working scenographers know how tempting it is to stick with those design solutions which have proved effective in the past, and how increasingly difficult it is to predict the success of a new idea. Undirected as this type of work might seem to be, it can have positive effects on a scenographer's future creations. For example, a piece of scrap electrical equipment can, when put into a relationship with the human figure, suggest two completely different possibilities to the scenographer's imagination, as shown in figures 107 and 108. In short, an integral part of the scenogra-

pher's craft must be a driving sensitivity to the entire world in which he lives; moreover, he must keep this sensitivity in constant operation: *the working scenographer works all the time.*

Much of the raw material of the scenographer's art is, of course, to be found in the various museums our civilization maintains; but that is not his exclusive source. And although most scenographers love those repositories which house the world's greatest cultural achievements, there must exist an equal passion for the more negative aspects of human accomplishment: the junkyard, the tenement, in fact, all the broken and discarded elements of our various cultures. Much of what we focus on in the theater takes place not with or within the finest examples of our art but in the derelict remains of our society. There should be, simply, no visual, tactile, or auditory phenomena outside the all-pervading attention of the scenographer. And while the selection of a play almost always precedes a design for it, the scenographer, in his day-to-day exposure to the world as a whole, should never miss the opportunity to let his imagination have free play, to "assign" a play or opera to a compelling visual image which might accidently capture that all-pervading attention. For instance, figure 109 shows the interior of a small freestanding fireplace which has been affected by years of use; its particular qualities might, to the discerning eye, provide an evocative scenic concept for a Greek play—perhaps *Electra*. It

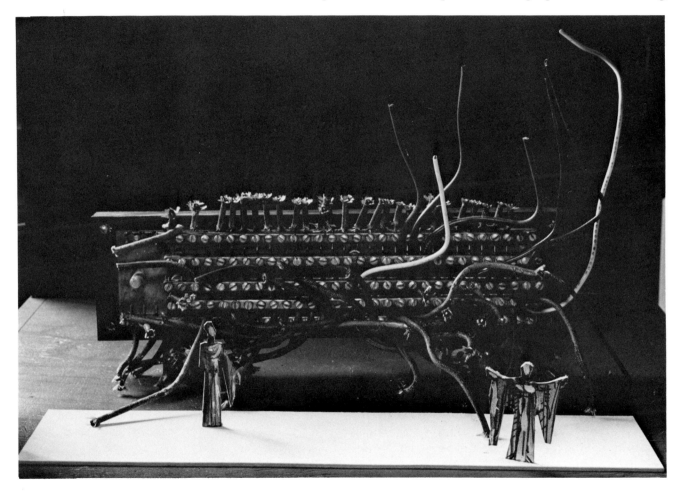

108. *Experimental
scenographic model
(variation)*

*109. Experimental
scenographic model*

even suggests an alternative plan to the usual placement of the permanent architectural features of such a play: the door to the palace might be put to one side (*A*) rather than in the center, its customary position.

The scenographer would do well to keep in mind Herman Melville's astute observation that "poetry is not a thing of ink and rhyme, but of thought and act, and, in the latter way, is by any one to be found anywhere, when in useful action sought."

12. Use of 35-mm Projection for Experimental Work

There are a number of ways the scenographer can use 35-mm slide projections. Not only do they allow him to record his productions for a permanent collection of past projects, they can also assist him in the creative process of designing a production. Perhaps it would be advantageous at this point to list the most important ways the 35-mm projection and projection equipment can be employed by the scenographer in his work before dealing with some of those categories in more depth.

1. To record the finished production most scenographers either have their work photographed or do it themselves. A 35-mm camera and projector are very wise investments for any scenographer, especially if he seeks research materials directly, as when traveling to a foreign country. It is also a wise precaution to have all models and finished sketches photographed in both black and white as well as in color. Most scenographers do not wish to incur the expense of sending large bulky portfolios to prospective employers; a careful selection of prints of models, set sketches, and production photos brought together in a careful presentation sells the scenographer much better than a bulging package of past work.

2. In the studio, highly evocative possibilities result from the projection of slides (of every sort and subject) on basic forms and textures. This process can be one of the most experimental and productive stages of the design exploration. It can also provide a positive form of creative play for the scenographer even when he has no specific project in mind; the results of this work might very well solve specific problems at a later time. (A more complete discussion of this process follows this outline.)

3. Images either selected or created can be photographed onto slides and used either as projections in the actual production or as an aid in duplicating them in a larger scale. (A more complete discussion of this process follows this outline.)

4. While we are not dealing with final renderings in this text, one method of making such a drawing (in lieu of traditional perspective drawing techniques) is to finish the model, photograph it onto a 35-mm slide,

and then project it onto a piece of blank white illustration board. This process makes it possible to trace
the outline in pencil with great accuracy. Figure 110
is a drawing made in this manner from the model
shown in figure 111.

Projection on Basic Forms and Surfaces

While it is not possible to outline completely all the
ways in which this experimentation might be con-
ducted, a few basic directions can be suggested here.
What causes differing effects will always be dependent, of course, on the surface onto which the images
are projected. These surfaces will in large part determine the quality and "message" of the image as perceived by an audience; scrims and other fabrics, gran-
ular surfaces, fractured forms, linear groupings, all
give markedly different effects. In figure 112 we have
a basic arrangement of forms. Figures 113 through
116 demonstrate how changed this same arrangement becomes when different images are projected
onto it.

But while many of the resulting designs created by
this method could be duplicated on the actual stage
with larger projectors than those used in the studio,
we are not limited to projections alone to secure the
final result; these experiments might very well serve
as the basis for determining designs which would be
painted on scenic units, not projected. Figure 117

*110. Photographic slide of
scenographic model*

111. *Scenographic sketch made from photographic slide*

shows a model composed of forms onto which an image has been projected; figure 118 is a similar model but the image, in this instance, has been painted directly on the forms. This method, then, provides the scenographer with interesting distortions which he could never "think" out on his own. One of the most positive reasons, in fact, why he should experiment with projects on his small model stage is that even the most inventive scenographer could never predict all the results obtainable by simple alteration in the distance, direction, and surface form to which an image may be subjected.

Use of Photographic Images in Full-Scale Scenic Painting

There is a relatively simple yet effective way by which a small preexisting image can be accurately duplicated on a larger scale. It is essentially the same process discussed above which demonstrated how an image of the scenic model could be used as a basis for making a scenographic sketch (see figs. 110, 111). The steps in the procedure recommended here are uncomplicated and can be mastered quickly. The following outline of these steps should explain the technique sufficiently.

1. Select desired image. Line drawings, such as the one used in the model shown in figure 119, give the best results, although the technique is not limited to this type of image alone. If the image is exceptionally

112. Basic scenographic model forms

113. *Projection on basic forms*

114. Projection on basic forms

115. *Projection on basic forms*

116. *Projection on basic forms*

117. *Experimental scenographic model*

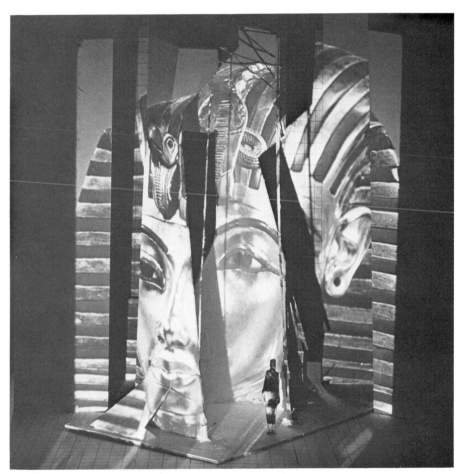

atmospheric, that is, if the lines of the objects and forms in it are indistinct, accurate duplication will of course be more difficult. Nevertheless, the basic scale and outline of the image can probably be better ascertained and more quickly laid out than when using the more customary grid of the painter's elevation.

2. A 35-mm slide must be made of the selected image. This slide must be extremely sharp and clear if the best results are to be obtained in the scene shop.

3. The slide can then be projected onto any prepared surface (fig. 120). The size of the image, naturally, will depend on how far the projector is from the surface of the scenic unit; a three-inch lens, however, gives a bigger image closer to the projection surface than will a five-inch lens. Since the size of the projected image is dependent on the distance from the projection surface, for large single works, such as a backdrop, it is advisable to divide the basic picture into segments, photographing each segment individually. Alignment of the separate parts back into the total image is not a difficult task if small key marks are made on the original picture.

4. It is a simple matter, even for those not trained in scene-painting technique, to follow the lines of the image with great accuracy. For larger images, where several painters might be required, it is wise to have them periodically trade off areas on which they are working. This is a practice that even professional scene painters use; it prevents the idiosyncrasies of paint-

118. Design derived from experimental model: Aïda, *tomb scene.*

119. *Image incorporated into model setting*

ing style, which no painter can avoid, from showing up too boldly in isolated areas. The general lighting of the area where the painting is to take place must, of course, be darker than when regular scene painting is being done. Figure 121 shows the finished unit in the actual setting.

5. This technique can also be used to project and duplicate distortions of the original image. This can be done by simply moving the projector to whatever angle gives the desired effect. Superimposition and multiple images may also be obtained by use of the projector. This can be done either by projecting the image onto the surface, painting it, and then projecting the second over the painted image. Using two projectors at once is possible, but it is often much more difficult to paint effectively the resulting image; the increased amount of light from the two projectors tends to fade both images to the point where accurate rendering of the painted image becomes a problem.

120. Technique for scenic painting of image

121. *Image duplicated in
actual setting:* As You
Like It

Part 4 *Photographing Scenographic Models*

13. Notes and Suggestions by Elliott Mendelson

The main problem in photographing model sets is creating the illusion of depth while maintaining a strong feeling for the dramatic impact desired by the scenographer. In this brief chapter, a few of the basic principles which have been developed over the past few years will be illustrated. It should be understood from the beginning that these are very basic principles and each photographic assignment may require slight modifications to achieve the best possible image.

The first step in making a model photograph is to discuss with the scenographer the various aspects of the set which are deemed important. From this discussion, a clearer understanding of motivation, direction, and personal feeling about the design can be discerned. Most scenographers will indicate a desire to re-create the impression one gets from seeing the actual set being used on a stage during a performance. While this can be achieved with much difficulty and expense, because of technical problems, a more direct approach to a single objective will prove just as beneficial. To this end decide whether the photograph is to be a record of the physical layout of the set's elements or a dramatic interpretation of the effects created by lighting.

What we see in black-and-white photographs is the sum total of all the images created by the bright and dark areas of the image. If in the model all the dark areas are eliminated (no shadows), the remaining image would be void of all form (fig. 122). If, on the other hand, the dark areas are increased to the point where one shadow intersects the other, the original forms would not be rendered accurately (fig. 123).

The first step in lighting a model is to provide separation between each of the set's elements by providing good lighting balance between the bright and the dark areas (contrast ratio [fig. 124]).

In figure 125 note that one light (fill) is located at the camera position. It is important that the quality of this light remain soft and produce no shadows on the set. The function of this lamp is to provide adequate illumination to record the image of the set on film. The softness of this lamp can be controlled by placing a translucent material in front of the light. By moving this defuser closer to the model, the quality of the light becomes softer. Once in place, a light meter reading can be made using the incident method to determine the proper exposure. Exposure and subsequent film development will be discussed later.

The next light to be placed is the key light. Unlike the fill light, the quality of light from this lamp should be harsh and produce marked shadows on the sets. It is this light source which will produce the separa- 137

122. *Flat-lighting effect:*
Cyrano de Bergerac

124. *Lighting for form*

tion between each of the major set elements. The position of this lamp is critical. Good separation can usually be obtained by placing this light source to the rear and to one side of the model. Elevate the lamp until the desired shadow length is achieved. Normally, the elevation of the lamp is such that it throws a beam of light at a 45-degree angle to the horizontal plane of the set. The intensity of this lamp should not be more than *one stop* greater than the fill light when both are measured using the incident method.

After some experimentation, satisfactory results should be obtainable in making a record photograph of the model using the two-light method described above. More dramatic effects are obtainable when: the contrast ratio between the key and fill light is increased; the angle of the key light is altered; or additional lighting equipment supplements the existing setup. One should be careful at this point not to add too many additional lights, as the shadows they produce will only tend to confuse rather than to add dramatic impact or clarify the final picture. One method used to enhance a particular area of the design is to reflect the light from one of the existing light sources off of a small piece of mirror. Strategically placed, several of these pinpoint light sources can add the dramatic impact desired by the scenographer or yourself. These mirrors can be permanently positioned on a small stick with sealing wax and then mounted to the table with plastic clay (fig. 126).

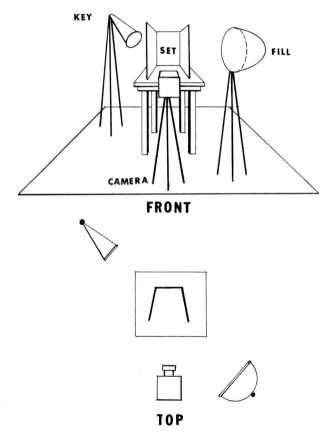

KEY   SET   FILL

CAMERA

FRONT

TOP

125. Diagram of lamp position

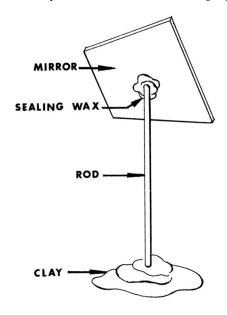

126. *Mirrors for spotlighting*

MIRROR

SEALING WAX

ROD

CLAY

There are several methods by which one can accurately determine the proper exposure for any type of photographic material. The best method requires a very selective spot meter and a good knowledge of Minor White's *Zone System Manual* (Dobbs Ferry, N.Y.: Morgan & Morgan, 1968). According to this method one would read the intensity of light being reflected only from the shadow areas where visible detail is desired in the final print. A second reading is then made from the brightest area of the model where detail is to be seen. The first of these two readings when reduced by 2 f-stops will provide the correct exposure.

Example: If your light meter indicates an exposure of ½ second at f-5.6, you would then close down the aperture of the lens 2 stops to f-11.

The second light meter reading (the one from the brightest area) is then compared with the f-stop and shutter speed used to expose the film. It is imperative that the shutter speeds of the two values being compared are identical.

Location of Meter Reading	Shutter Speed	F-Stop
Exposure for shadow area less 2 stops	½ sec.	11
Exposure indicated for brightest area	½ sec.	64

When compared, the difference is 5 f-stops (16, 22, 32, 45, 65). This value represents the contrast ratio between the shadows and the highlight areas. If the ratio is 5 f-stops, normal development of the film is suggested. If the ratio is 1 stop more or less than 5 f-stops, the development time should be reduced 20 percent or increased 20 percent respectively.

Difference between Highest and Lowest F-Stop Reading	Development Time
4 stops	normal and 20 percent of normal
5 stops	normal
6 stops	normal and 20 percent of normal

There are many times when it is not practical to develop your own film. On these occasions it is recommended that the fill-light position be altered by moving it closer to or further from the model to alter the contrast ratio. In this way a commercial film processor can develop the film normally, and good highlight detail can be retained.

A simpler, but not as accurate, method to determine proper film exposure is by using an incident light meter. For most amateurs the incident method will give satisfactory results for both color and black-and-white films. Unlike the reflected meter-reading method, the incident meter is pointed toward the camera from the position of the model and measures the amount of light radiated from the lamps. The major disadvantage to this method is the fact that no allowance is made for the particular absorption qualities of the pigments used in painting the model. Thus any exposure determined by this method might be as much as 2 f-stops greater or lower than the one needed to obtain good shadow detail. For this reason it is

recommended that the photographer bracket his exposures to compensate for this deficiency.

Example: If your meter indicates an exposure of ½ second at f-8, then expose 5 separate frames, one at each of the following f-stops while retaining the same shutter speed: 4, 5.6, 8, 11, 16.

A simple test for the contrast ratio can be made by comparing the intensities of the fill and key lights. As in the first method, the comparison should be made between the two different aperture readings when the shutter speeds remain constant. The proper developing time for the film is then as described in the first method illustrated above.

While almost any camera can be used to record the model's image, a 4-by-5-inch view camera with swings and tilts is highly recommended. Without the use of perspective corrections available on a view camera, the vertical lines of the model will keystone when the view axis of the camera is not perpendicular to the model's vertical planes. A similar experience can be observed when the camera is not perpendicular to the horizontal plane. Additionally, the swings and tilts of the lens plane of the camera will afford the photographer greater control over the field desired to be in focus.

Lens usage is normally a subjective choice made by the photographer; depending on the purpose of the photograph almost any lens can do the job. When

127. *Camera elevation*

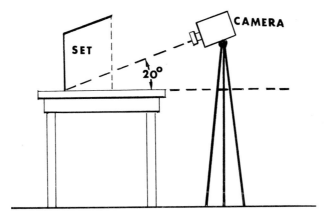

making record shots of models, a 210-mm lens on a 4-by-5-inch camera is normally employed. Compared to other lenses for the same size format, a 210-mm lens is considered a short telephoto. For other camera formats, see the table below.

Format	Lens
35 mm	90 mm
2¼ by 2¼ inches	135 mm or 150 mm

The lenses indicated above will record the model nearly as the mind's eye sees it. Shorter focal length lenses will allow the camera to get closer to the model, resulting in seemingly exaggerated relationships between the elements. Longer focal length lenses tend to compress the elements of the model and diminish size relationships.

When a 4-by-5-inch camera is not available and your camera has no perspective controls, the keystoning which results on your negative can be corrected to some degree when the negative is printed. Some loss in quality should be expected as well as some loss of the negative's original image.

The most common mistake made in photographing both model sets and actual sets being used in production is the point of view. From your discussions with the scenographer it will probably become apparent that some sense of dimension is desirable. If the camera angle relative to the stage floor is too low, all sense of depth is lost. On the other hand, if the camera angle is too high then the full impact of the set's elements is lost. For most general and record-type photography, an angle of 20 to 35 degrees, when measured between the plane of the stage floor and a line intersecting the plane of the stage floor from the rear of the set to the camera lens, seems to work best (fig. 127).

Photographing Model Sets

1. Position the fill light and its diffuser at the camera position.

2. Position the key light behind, above, and to one side of the model.

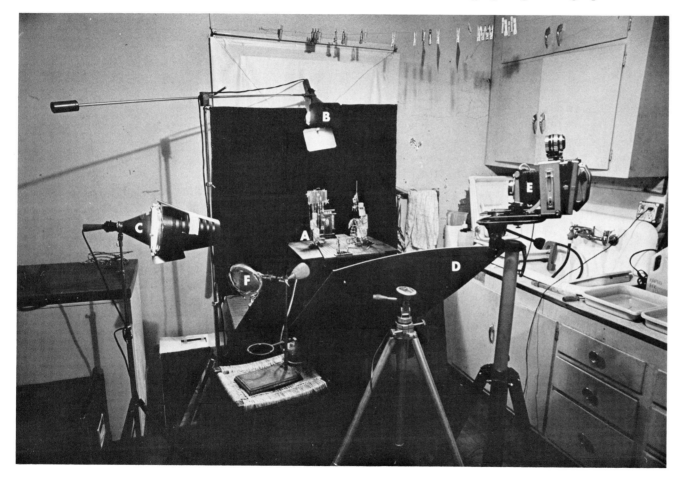

129. *Result of setup:* The Skin of Our Teeth, *act 1.*

3. Set the camera at an angle of 20 to 35 degrees to the set.

4. Add additional lights and/or reflectors for dramatic effect.

5. Use a short telephoto lens on the camera.

6. Determine the proper exposure for good shadow detail.

7. Calculate the contrast ratio for film development.

8. If using a 4-by-5-inch camera, set wings and tilts for parallel vertical planes.

9. Set the lens aperture for the amount of field desired in focus.

10. Always use a tripod.

Figure 128 is a typical setup for the photographing of a scenographic model. The various elements in the setup are (*A*) model subject, (*B*) key light, (*C*) special sidelight, (*D*) reflective fill-light board, (*E*) camera on tripod, (*F*) mirror. Figure 129 shows the final result of this particular setup.

NOTE: While photographing scenographic models in the studio is a necessity in most instances, it is possible to use actual sunlight as the primary source of light (fig. 130). This practice, at best, has limited value; however, many scenographers in the early years of this century—Gordon Craig for one—did have their models photographed out-of-doors. Experimentation with natural light is encouraged especially for the amateur photographer.

130. Use of natural light for photographing scenographic model

Annotated Bibliography
Index

Annotated Bibliography

The purpose of this brief bibliography is not scholarly; what it does present, however, is a small number of books which, it is reasonable to assume, would be in any fair-sized university library and which contain a broad spectrum of approaches to the making of model settings. There are many more books that do contain some models, even giving information as to their construction. Most of these books have not been included here, since the instruction they give is too brief or rudimentary; in any case, what they do show will have been covered in the main body of this book. The greatest source of recently completed models will, of course, appear in the various theater journals which appear monthly, bimonthly, or quarterly. Nevertheless, although there are a great number of publications being offered continually, few deal directly with scenographic design or individual scenographers. And even of those only *Theatre Crafts* and *Theatre and Technology* consistently show the current work—including models—of practicing scenographers. Foreign publications, such as *Tabs*, *Theater Heute*, and *Theatre in Poland*, tend to be rich in pictorial materials and sometimes do, but not often, include photographs of models in their articles on production. Most periodical publications dealing with theater can be, as with individual books, found in most university libraries.

The student of scenography should not, however, limit his attention to theater publications alone; he should also keep well abreast of the developments in related fields of art as well. Not only should he be familiar with those works to be found in single books dealing with individual artists and movements, he should also give his continuing attention to periodical publications, such as *Art Forum*, *Art in America*, and *Craft Horizons*, which help both the artist and public keep up with the ever-changing trends in the various arts and crafts of our period. These publications are especially recommended to the scenographer, since they expose and explain new concepts, materials, and techniques which have a direct bearing on the manner in which the scenic work of the modern theater is conceived and realized.

Art and the Stage in Twentieth Century. Edited by Henning Rischbieter, documented by Wolfgang Storch. Greenwich, Conn.: New York Graphic Society, 1970.

This book, which carries the subtitle *Painters and Sculptors Work for the Theater*, does, indeed, show the work of artists who are not primarily scenographers. The reason it is mentioned here is twofold; first, it does contain twenty-eight models for stage settings, utilizing a wide spectrum of materials and techniques, and second, the work it represents gives the more traditional practice of scenography some highly evocative directions. It should come as no surprise that while the painters included in the book tend toward pictorial and essentially "painterly" settings, the sculptors are more sensitive to the three-dimensional qualities inherent in scenography. For this reason, the sculptors—like Alexander Calder, Fritz Wortuba, and Giacomo Manzu—seem to be more in tune with designs found in today's theater than do the painters. In fact, the sculptors appear to strive much more to make their work part of the total production than do the painters who, unfortunately, tend to remain their own graphically forceful selves. Nevertheless, this is a book which should be carefully studied by all students of scenography; and while a great deal of its interest is unquestionably historical, much of what is included can suggest to the present-day scenographer new and innovative approaches to his own work.

Bablet, Denis. *Edward Gordon Craig*. London: Heinemann Educational Books, 1966.

This book, primarily historical in content, contains only five model photographs; they do, however, adequately demonstrate Craig's use of them in his work. These models, and others of Craig's, are definite forerunners for most scenographers of the twentieth century; in both form and spirit they foreshadow much of the work of Josef Svoboda. (Svoboda, like Craig, often employs bold shadow patterns on massively scaled modular units to define the stage space for a specific scene.) Comparison of Craig's models for *Hamlet* with those of Svoboda's demonstrates a strikingly similar approach in both conception and style.

———. *Revolution in Stage Design of the XXth Century*. Paris and New York: Leon Amiel, 1977.

This excellent book contains fifty-nine models spanning some eighty years and nearly every country. But it also contains a wealth of other visual materials from twentieth-century theater practice; for an overview of the entire period, this work will be difficult to match. I do not know of any other work on the subject of scenography that gives so complete a picture in one text or that illustrates the subject better. It is highly recommended for the scenographer's personal library and is a wise investment for both academic and professional scenographers.

Burian, Jarka. *The Scenography of Josef Svoboda*. Middletown, Conn.: Wesleyan University Press, 1971.

Svoboda makes an extensive use of models in his work, especially in the experimental stage. Most of his models are highly finished works, often containing mechanized working parts which correspond to the machinery used in their actual production on the stage. The materials he employs in constructing these models are usually more durable than most modelmakers use; they are also constructed by artisans who have cabinetmaking skills and sophisticated tools at their disposal. The book contains forty-three photographs of models, although some are multiple views and variations of a single model. This is an extremely valuable book and should be in the permanent library of all scenographers.

Contemporary Stage Design—U.S.A. Edited by Elizabeth Burdick, Peggy C. Hansen, and Brenda Zanger. International Institute of the United States, Inc. Middletown, Conn.: Wesleyan University Press, 1974.

This catalogue contains eighteen models; it provides a good overall view of scenographic practice in the United

States during the first part of the 1970s, both in professional as well as in university theater. Most of the models are of the exhibition type and several are reproduced in exceptionally fine color.

Friedman, Martin. *Hockney Paints the Stage*. New York: Abbeville Press (with The Walker Art Center, Minneapolis, Minn.), 1983.

The title tells all. Nevertheless, while David Hockney is first and resolutely foremost a painter using the stage as a large canvas, he does extend his graphic skills sufficiently to produce carefully drawn and painted models. This book contains fifteen of those models, all shown in color. Like Picasso and many other painters before him, Hockney is not a scenographer per se, but is—again like Picasso—lured into the theater from time to time precisely charged to exhibit his own idiosyncratic vision. Nor would it be unfair to say that those who have provided him with opportunities to apply his skills to theatrical production are much less concerned with the appropriateness of that collaboration than they are with the exploitation of a well-known name from another art form. And it is entirely justified to level the same charge against Hockney that the noted ballet critic Richard Buckle made concerning another famous painter of the past, Salvador Dali: "It must be quite clear to anyone looking at . . . Dali's curtain and *décor* for *Mad Tristan* that the celebrated Catalan illusionist does not design ballets—he allows dancers to take part in his paintings." Still, study of this book will give a good idea of how forceful (and how potentially dangerous to a performer) painted scenery can be when not integrated with all other elements of the theater.

Fuerst, Walter René, and Samuel J. Hume. *Twentieth-Century Stage Design*. 2 vols. New York: Dover Publications, 1967.

These two volumes (vol. 1, text, vol. 2, illustrations) were first published by Alfred A. Knopf in 1929. They have, however, been brought out again in an inexpensive paperbook format by the publisher listed above. There are thirty-eight models in volume 2; those shown—in addition to all the other types of work included—are of especial value to the scenographer studying the varied trends of scenography during this period, a period which very much forms the basis of our own. This two-volume set provides a good international view of designs from a period which was extremely active and revolutionary in the art of scenography. The relatively small cost of this set recommends it for the scenographer's personal library.

Hainaux, René. *Stage Design throughout the World since 1935*. New York: Theatre Arts Books, 1957.

This is the first of four books showing a representative collection from a number of countries of designs created since 1935. While the greater number of the works shown are sketches and drawings, thirty-two models showing a wide range of different approaches are included.

―――. *Stage Design throughout the World since 1950*. New York: Theatre Arts Books, 1964.

The second in the series shows designs from various countries with Austria, Bulgaria, Canada, Cuba, East Germany, Hungary, India, Israel, Peru, Rumania, Spain, Turkey, USSR, Uruguay, and Venezuela participating for the first time. Again, there are more sketches than models; but the number of models does increase to thirty-eight. There is also a short section in this book, which the first did not contain, that gives the views of scenographers concerning the use of new materials in their designs along with comments about their particular methods of work and philosophies of production. This information is helpful in showing the trends away from painted pictorial settings and toward the more sculptural three-dimensional aspects of present-day scenography.

―――. *Stage Design throughout the World since 1960*. New York: Theatre Arts Books, 1972.

In the third book of this series, the number of models has increased to fifty-eight (which supports the contention made early in the present volume that models are becoming a more popular form of presentation among scenographers). In addition, the approaches to the construction of the individual models varies much more than in the earlier two books. The various trends which began to manifest themselves in the second of the series become more prominent from 1960 on; scenographers are using the three-dimensional model to indicate radical spatial arrangements and newer materials which would not be as evident in a flat scenic sketch. The student of scenography can, from the study of these three books, obtain a fairly accurate overview of the predominant features of scenography as it has developed—as the title of the series indicates—throughout the world during the past forty years. The complete set, although expensive, is recommended as a wise investment for the personal library of all scenographers.

―――. *Stage Design throughout the World 1970–75*. New York: Theatre Arts Books, 1976.

In the fourth book of this series (and representing the shortest span of time of all four volumes), the number of models shown has dropped significantly to eighteen. However, the reason for this low number has less to do with the shorter time period or a decreasing use of scenographic models than it does with the increasingly disturbing trend—for this series of books at least—toward reproducing sensational close-up photographs of individual performers and small groups taken during performance. All in all, this last volume is a disappointment to those interested in examining the work of scenographers during the period of time selected. It is to be hoped that future issues in this series will return to the basic purpose stated in the title of the series and will devote less space to images which, while interesting as pictures of a performer's gesture, do not serve the scenographer who would appreciate wider more comprehensive views of the productions selected as outstanding examples of world scenography. While this book does not represent the best features of the other three, it still should be considered as an integral part of the series and for that reason alone is recommended for the scenographer's personal library.

Hohauser, Sanford. *Architectural and Interior Models, Design and Construction*. New York: Van Nostrand Reinhold, 1970.

This is probably the most complete book in print on architectural model construction. Nevertheless, it is of limited use to the scenographic model builder; the tools, level of skills, materials, and ultimate purpose of architectural model building go far beyond the necessities of the stage and well beyond the resources of the average scenographic studio. While scenographic models can take several days or—at the most—a few weeks to complete, often costing less than ten to fifteen dollars at the outside, an architectural model, such as the ones demonstrated in this book, may take many highly skilled workmen months to complete, take up several square yards of space, and cost tens of thousands of dollars. This book is recommended, however, since it gives thorough lists of materials, techniques, and tools available to modelmakers, as well as sources for supplies and highly specialized equipment. What it has to say about modelmaking for the stage is minimal and less than informative (only one page and one poorly constructed model is included in the entire text). But it

is an interestingly detailed look into the possibilities of this rather unique activity. The book is now issued in paperback and remains relatively inexpensive; for this reason it is recommended for the scenographer's personal library.

Kuh, Katharine. *Break-Up*. Greenwich, Conn.: New York Graphic Society, 1965.

In many ways, this book is the student's best introduction to the art of the past century. In it the author quickly traces the most important developments of the twentieth-century approach to all the visual arts, with a minimum amount of verbiage. Her commentary relates directly to the problems faced by the present-day scenographer.

Osborne, Charles. *The World Theatre of Wagner*. New York: Macmillian, 1982.

While this book contains few models, it is such a complete visual record of both historical and contemporary approaches to the production of Wagner's operas that it is a highly recommended addition to any scenographer's personal library. The many photographs—a great number in exceptionally fine color—of actual productions along with a generous number of scenographic drawings amply demonstrate the unusually wide diversity of styles imposed on Wagner's work. Without doubt this book will prove a valuable research source to any practicing scenographer whether he actually works in the operatic theater or is interested in transferring the stagecraft of the opera stage to other theatrical forms.

Pecktal, Lynn. *Designing and Painting for the Theatre*. New York: Holt, Rinehart & Winston, 1975.

To date, this is the best book yet available to American students of scenography concerning the technical practices currently used in the professional theater and in the scenic shops—primarily those in New York—which serve this level of theater. Pecktal has also provided a fairly clear picture of the type of work required from the scenographer working in that particular arena. In studying this book it becomes increasingly clear that modelmaking is a practical necessity for most present-day scenographers. A number of models, thirty-two in all, are included in this book, as well as is a three-page outline of materials and techniques employed in modelmaking. Since this book is an extremely valuable collection of specific information, it is highly recommended as an addition to the permanent library of all scenographers.

Rubin, William S. *Dada and Surrealist Art*. New York: Harry N. Abrams, 1969.

This book deals with an extremely important aspect of twentieth-century art and much of what is presented has directly influenced all arts of the theater for the past fifty years. This is a work which should be in the permanent library of the scenographer.

Seitz, William C. *The Art of Assemblage*. Museum of Modern Art. Garden City, N.Y.: Doubleday, 1961.

This is an excellent book which traces the historical development of the whole art of assemblage and collage; the text is accompanied by an extensive collection of examples.

Warre, Michael. *Designing and Making Stage Scenery*. London: Studio Vista; New York: Reinhold Publishers, 1966.

This book contains eleven models, mostly by British scenographers, and has several good color reproductions. The text of this book, however, gives little practical professional information about any phase of scenography.

Wescher, Herta. *Collage*. Translated by Robert E. Wolf. New York: Harry N. Abrams, 1968.

This book deals with three-dimensional work while emphasizing the development of the flat assembly of textures, found images, and colors. Since much of scenography depends on assembly of similar materials, this book is recommended for careful study.

Index

Index

Darwin Reid Payne is an adjunct professor in theater at Wake Forest University at Winston-Salem, North Carolina. He was formerly chairman of the Theater Department of Southern Illinois University at Carbondale. In addition to designing and directing at regional theaters throughout the United States and Canada, he is also writing a study of the use of metaphorical imagery in scenography and theatrical direction.